The Christian Faith

"In this volume, renowned Lutheran theologian Carl Braaten sifts through two millennia of Christian wisdom, all the while in conversation with contemporary challenges to faith, in order to offer a compelling restatement of fundamental Christian truths. Passionate for both the gospel and the church, he offers a compelling ecumenical engagement readable for clergy and laity alike. If you are not already an 'Evangelical Catholic,' Braaten will persuade you to become one."

—Mark C. Mattes, Professor of Theology and Philosophy, Grand View University

"Carl Braaten offers in this book a clear, succinct, scholarly, and widely ecumenical study of the Christian faith. As a dogmatic study, it faithfully draws from the fountain of the Holy Scriptures and the church creeds in an objective and open ecumenical dialogue. He engages constructively the Roman Catholic Church, the Protestant, Evangelical, and Pentecostal churches, as well as the main world religions in an effort to strengthen and rejuvenate the trinitarian mission of the one, holy, catholic, and apostolic church. I recommend this book highly as a resource for the formation of lay church leaders, seminarians, continuing education of pastors, and textbook in introduction to theology courses."

—Alberto L. García, co-author of *Wittenberg Meets The World: Reimagining the Reformation at the Margins*

"Carl Braaten once again leads Evangelical Catholics—those who love both Christ's gospel and his body, the church—into new territory that is also very ancient: the common ground of an ecumenical theology for the whole church. Pastors, teachers, and learners from a variety of church traditions will find the essentials of Christian faith set forth here in brief and useful form, in Braaten's characteristically clear and vigorous prose."

—Philip Cary, editor of *Pro Ecclesia: A Journal of Catholic and Evangelical Theology*

"Professor Braaten's lucid and refreshing summary of the Christian faith reflects more than six decades of teaching theology. With impressive command of the relevant literature, especially the Holy Scriptures and the classic creeds and confessions, and with deep understanding of the dogmatic consensus in the current ecumene, Braaten here offers a stimulating defense of the faith that is properly orthodox, catholic, and evangelical. This master teacher goes to the heart of what is essential."

—Matthew L. Becker, Professor of Theology, Valparaiso University

"For pastors who need a word to renew their preaching and teaching as well as for seminarians whose vocational callings are just being shaped, *The Christian Faith* will serve as an orientation to theological thinking moving us beyond the veneers of partisan and sectarian boundaries towards the common future into which God is drawing us. Dr. Braaten's clear and crisp writing is a classic example of the way in which the discipline of dogmatics draws us into the truth as it gives the reader both explanation and faithful testimony rooted in the apostolic witness and the trinitarian structure of the creeds."

—Amy C. Schifrin, President, North American Lutheran Seminary

The Christian Faith
—— *Ecumenical Dogmatics* ——

Carl E. Braaten

To
The Center for Catholic and Evangelical Theology
and
PRO ECCLESIA
A Journal of Catholic and Evangelical Theology

CASCADE *Books* • Eugene, Oregon

THE CHRISTIAN FAITH
Ecumenical Dogmatics

Copyright © 2020 Carl E. Braaten. All rights reserved. Except for brief quotations in critical publications or reviews, no part of this book may be reproduced in any manner without prior written permission from the publisher. Write: Permissions, Wipf and Stock Publishers, 199 W. 8th Ave., Suite 3, Eugene, OR 97401.

Cascade Books
An Imprint of Wipf and Stock Publishers
199 W. 8th Ave., Suite 3
Eugene, OR 97401

www.wipfandstock.com

PAPERBACK ISBN: 978-1-7252-5146-5
HARDCOVER ISBN: 978-1-7252-5147-2
EBOOK ISBN: 978-1-7252-5148-9

Cataloguing-in-Publication data:

Names: Braaten, Carl E., author.

Title: The Christian faith : ecumenical dogmatics / by Carl E. Braaten.

Description: Eugene, OR: Cascade Books, 2020 | Includes bibliographical references.

Identifiers: ISBN 978-1-7252-5146-5 (paperback) | ISBN 978-1-7252-5147-2 (hardcover) | ISBN 978-1-7252-5148-9 (ebook)

Subjects: LCSH: Theology—Doctrinal.

Classification: BT77 .B745 2020 (print) | BT77 .B745 (ebook)

Manufactured in the U.S.A.   05/11/20

Contents

Introduction | ix

1. **The Holy Scriptures** | 1
   Scripture and Tradition   2
   The Authority of Holy Scripture   3
   The Interpretation of Scripture   5

2. **The Holy Trinity** | 9
   Trinitarian Heresies   10
   Renewal of Trinitarian Theology   12
   Trinity and Church   14

3. **The Knowledge of God** | 18
   The Special Revelation of God   18
   Law and Gospel   20
   No Other Name   21
   Natural Knowledge of God   23

4. **God the Creator** | 26
   Creation Out of Nothing   26
   Theodicy   27
   Creationism Versus Evolution   28
   Gnostic Dualism   29
   Ethics of the Body   30

5. Sin, Death, and the Devil | 33

The Nature and Effects of Sin   33
New Testament Concepts of Sin   36
Original and Hereditary Sin   37
Pelagian and Manichaean Heresies   39
The Destiny of Death   42
The Devil, Enemy of God   45

6. The Person of Christ | 50

What Is Christology?   50
The Life and Ministry of Jesus   52
Death and Resurrection   53
The Divine Identity of Jesus of Nazareth   56
Christological Heresies   58
The Two Natures of Christ   60

7. The Work of Christ | 65

The New Testament and Mythology   65
The Preexistence of Christ   67
The Virgin Birth   67
The Cross of Christ   70
Theories of the Atonement   72
Descent Into Hell   74
The Resurrection   75
The Ascension and Session at the Right Hand of the Father   79
The Return of Christ   81

8. The Holy Spirit | 83

Controversies About the Holy Spirit   83
The Person and Work of the Holy Spirit   86

9. The Church | 90

    The Nature of the Church   91

    The One, Holy, Catholic, and Apostolic Church   91

    Marks of the Church   95

    The Offices of Ministry   97

10. The Word and Sacraments | 101

    The External Word   101

    The Law and Gospel of God   102

    The Sacraments   104

    Baptism   106

    The Lord's Supper   109

11. The Church and the World | 114

    The Doctrine of Justification   114

    The Economy   120

    Sex, Marriage, and Family   124

12. The Christian Mission and World Religions | 130

    Ecumenism and Mission   131

    The Pluralistic Theory of Religions   133

    Preparation for the Gospel   136

    Interpretation of Religions Other Than Christian   137

13. Eschatology: The Christian Hope | 143

    Resurrection of the Dead   145

    Rethinking Traditional Eschatology   146

    Hope and Universal Salvation   150

    The Last Judgment   155

Bibliography | 157

Index | 161

Introduction

We are fortunate to be living in an ecumenical age. This situation was underscored by the Second Vatican Council, convoked in Rome in 1962 by Pope John XXIII, and closed in 1965. The ecumenical factor beckons us to think and act out of a new vision of doing theology in such a way that we do not merely repristinate our confessional catechisms or partisan polemics. The experience of participating in the ecumenical dialogues and studying the many declarations that participating churches have subscribed is shared by millions of Christians—Evangelicals, Catholics, and Orthodox. In spite of the fact that the major Christian churches do not agree on every doctrine, they now for the most part call each other "brothers and sisters in Christ." With some regrettable exceptions most churches welcome each others' members to join them in prayer and worship, and their ministers often preach in each others' pulpits and preside at each others' altars. Theologians from across the ecumenical spectrum read each others' books and benefit from what other churches believe and teach on the basis of the Bible and the ancient creeds. In doing this they become better equipped to challenge the demonic ideologies rampant in contemporary culture and the destructive heresies and apostasies that circulate within Christianity today.

Ecumenical dogmatics gives preeminent priority to the Holy Scriptures of the Old and New Testaments and the ancient creeds of the church, especially the Apostles' Creed, the Nicene-Constantinopolitan Creed of 381 AD, and the Athanasian Creed (ca. late fifth century). Another very important creed is from the Council of Chalcedon, 451 AD. These creeds define the orthodox Christian teaching on the Holy Trinity, Father, Son, and Holy Spirit, equally of the same being (*homoousious*), and of the person of Jesus Christ, truly God and truly man. The Apostles' Creed and the Athanasian Creed originated in the West under the influence of the Church of Rome, and are accepted by the Roman Catholic Church and mainline Protestant churches, Lutheran, Reformed, and Anglican. Only the Nicene-Constantinopolitan

INTRODUCTION

Creed is truly an ecumenical creed, accepted by both Eastern and Western branches of Christianity. Lorenzo Valla, an Italian humanist and historian in the fifteenth century, proved that the Apostles' Creed was not written by the first-century apostles and the Athanasian Creed was not written by St. Athanasius in the fourth century. The Apostles' Creed dates back to the fifth or sixth century in southern France and developed from an ancient Roman creed used in the liturgy of baptism. Nevertheless, the Apostles' Creed contains articles of faith that were current in the churches by the end of the first century, articulated by bishops and presbyters who were disciples of the apostles.

The creeds were deemed necessary in the ancient church for several reasons. First, they provided clear summaries of what the church believes and teaches, based on the Holy Scriptures, and that proved to be pedagogically useful in catechesis and the baptismal liturgy. Second, the creeds provided the key to interpret the Bible in the right way. They possess hermeneutical significance to this day. *Hermeneutics* is a word that stems from the name of the Greek god, Hermes, the messenger god who carried messages between the Olympian deities. Thus, hermeneutics is the fine art of interpreting ancient texts, carrying their message into the present-day context so that recipients can better understand what is written. Some Protestant churches were told by their founders not to use the creed, guided by the slogan, "No creed but Christ!" Their motive was to bring about Christian unity, since the denominations seemed to be divided by their separate confessions. The danger is that generations later they run the risk of ending up with neither creed nor Christ. And that leads to greater division than ever. Significant ecumenical progress toward Christian unity has been achieved by those denominations that subscribe to the ancient creeds of the church. Their dialogues are theologically rich and promising.

The Protestant churches of the Reformation kept the ancient creeds of the church. The Reformers had no intention of inventing a new Christianity or teaching anything contrary to the Holy Scriptures and the doctrines of the church catholic of the first five centuries. For them the purpose of the creeds is evangelical, to placard Christ and keep his gospel front and center in everything the church teaches and preaches. In the meantime the term *Protestant* has become problematic; it has come to mean almost everything and nearly nothing. Some liberal Protestant churches make up new creeds, omitting the parts of the old creeds they deem outdated and unbelievable, like the divinity of Christ, the virgin birth, or resurrection of the body. Many recovering Protestants prefer to self-identify as "evangelical catholics," in distinction from Eastern Catholics (Orthodox) and Roman Catholics. All three claim to be members of the one, holy, catholic, and apostolic church of the triune God. The word *evangelical* stems from the "evangel," the good news of the gospel. Evangelical catholics intend by their confession to remain faithful to the mainstream of the classical Christian tradition, as formulated in its major creeds. The word *catholic* means universal in extent, involving all. Either a church is catholic or it is a sect. Theologians who cherish the creeds use them as a map that instructs them how best to travel to a distant country with a strange language. To interpret the Bible without the creed is like taking a trip without a map. Those who ignore the creeds of the church tend to get lost by reading their own personal views into the Bible, possibly producing a sect, be it that of Mary Baker Eddy, Joseph Smith, or Charles Russell.

A silent struggle is going on in modern theology between two opposing ways of thinking about the Christian faith and doctrine. The two types are commonly referred to as "revisionist" and "confessionalist." They treat the creedal deposits of the common Christian tradition differently. A revisionist tends to revise the traditional statements of faith in accord with post-Enlightenment modernity and personal religious experience. The ancient creeds and doctrines are understood as the expression of the religious experiences of pre-modern times, and therefore lack binding authority on present-day religious communities. The father of this revisionist line of expressing the Christian faith is Friedrich Schleiermacher (1768–1834). This approach accounts for the rise of radical pluralism in modern theology, conforming to the many varieties of religious experience.

The confessionalist approach advocates a method of dogmatics that treats doctrines as the church's reflection on the Word of God in its three forms, the incarnate Word (Christ), the written Word (Bible), and the preached Word (sermon). Preachers have been called and ordained by their respective churches to proclaim the Word of God, not words about their religious experience or political ideology. A good sermon gives voice to what God has revealed in the biblical story of salvation, with Christ as its center. In the confessionalist approach to teaching the doctrines of the Christian faith, experience does play an essential role, but not as the source of Christian truth. Experience is the subjective medium that receives the saving message arising from the sources of revelation. The sources are given by God in the history of salvation, starting with the election of Israel in the Old Testament, culminating with Jesus Christ in the New Testament, and continuing with the apostles and evangelists who turned the Mediterranean world upside down, planting churches throughout the Roman Empire. Confesionalists do not make up a new Christianity to rhyme with their subjective feelings about anything.

Dorothy Sayers was an English playwright, poet, author of mysteries, and Christian essayist. In her book, *Creed or Chaos? Why Christians Must Choose Either Dogma or Disaster*, she wrote that it is a lie to say that dogma (the creed) does not matter; it matters enormously. She said it is fatal to let people suppose that Christianity is only a mode of feeling and that not one person in a hundred has the faintest notion what the church teaches about God or the person of Jesus Christ. For the revisionists, doctrines are non-informative symbols of inner feelings, attitudes, and experiences. New doctrines develop as traditional symbols and metaphors are modernized to express new experiences of ourselves, God, and the world.

The modern ecumenical movement would not have been productive if the revisionists would have been in charge of the many dialogues that have taken place among the participating churches. The dialogue teams were generally composed of theologians faithfully representative of their own confessional standards. This accounts for their amazing grace-filled openness toward one another, creating a new climate of hospitality of churches toward each other across the world. It would take a learned historian to tell the whole story of the many factors that have indirectly contributed to the new ecumenical consciousness in world Christianity, factors such as the persecution of Christians, the demise of Christendom, the increase of anti-Christian enemies, the rise of secularism in traditional Christian nations, and the decline of membership in all mainline denominations. All these factors have made churches of all confessions aware of their beleaguered status. In similar circumstances the biblical prophets told the people of Israel not to lose hope; God is still in charge. The invisible hand of God, the Lord of history, is at work behind the backs of all the "powers and principalities" of this *age* to bring his enslaved people home to the promised land. The same hidden God

INTRODUCTION

of history is at work today, using even the enemies of Christianity as agents to turn the churches away from false securities and return to the essentials of the Christian faith, based on the biblical, creedal, liturgical, and sacramental truths and practices common to them all.

The core of such ecclesial truths and practices is the revelation of God in Jesus Christ. Every Christian community since ancient times has claimed that its doctrines express the true faith of the one church of Christ, and that they are not aberrant teachings of a sect. Every church tradition tends to emphasize a particular aspect of the "great tradition." Lutherans, for example, typically stress the doctrine of justification by faith alone (*sola fide*), because they believe it expresses the heart of God's saving revelation in Christ. They would make the same claim about the other *solas*—*sola scriptura* and *sola gratia*. "Scripture *alone*," "grace *alone*," and "faith *alone*" might give credence to the charge that the Lutheran confession is guilty of reductionism, affirming Scripture without tradition, grace without faith, or faith without works. That would be a twisted misunderstanding. The "*solas*" combine to affirm that God has revealed himself definitively in Christ alone (*solus Christus*) and not through any other mediators, whether it be Mohammed, Buddha, Lao-tzu, Joseph Smith, Mary Baker Eddy, or Sun Myung.

Libraries contain a plethora of dogmatics—Evangelical, Reformed, Lutheran, Catholic, or Orthodox. My former professor of dogmatics at the University of Heidelberg, Edmund Schlink, was bold enough to write an "*Ecumenical Dogmatics*." Church dogmaticians strive to be faithful to the canon formulated by Vincent of Lérins, a fifth century monk, that "all possible care should be taken that we hold that faith which has been believed everywhere, always and by all."[1] The one thing that all Christians and all churches in all times and places share is the divinely revealed gospel of Jesus Christ according to the Scriptures. The Apostle Paul summarized the gospel in 1 Corinthians 15:3–6.

> For I delivered to you as of first importance what I also received, that Christ died for our sins in accordance with the Scriptures, that he was buried, that he was raised on the third day in accordance with the scriptures, and that he appeared to Cephas, then to the twelve.

---

1. *Quod ubique, quod semper, quod ab omnibus.*

INTRODUCTION

What is unique about God's revelation in Jesus Christ is the person himself. The apostolic conviction expressed in the Nicene Creed that Jesus is "true God from true God" and "of one Being with the Father" is the root of the doctrine of the Holy Trinity. Take that away and the trinitarian doctrine collapses into some kind of unitarianism. The revelation of God in Jesus Christ is the gospel of the triune God *according to the Scriptures*. The phrase "according to the Scriptures" is just as important for Catholics and Orthodox as for Evangelicals. There is broad ecumenical agreement that the Bible conveys the Word of God that creates the church. At the same time the Bible is the church's book. Where there is no church the Bible would not be acknowledged as the Word of God and there would be no need for it. Without the Bible the church has nothing to proclaim to the world; without the church the Bible is a mere collection of ancient documents with no more authority than the Hindu Upanishads. It is solely on account of Christ that all churches accept the authority of the Bible. Luther's dictum, *Was Christus treibt*,[2] expresses what all churches implicitly practice. Their sermons and commentaries demonstrate that Christ is the hinge on which everything else depends.

Dogmatics is a discipline of Christian theology that explains the doctrinal truths of faith promulgated by the councils of the church. Dogmatics became a highly specialized discipline of theology in the nineteenth century, among Lutheran, Reformed, and Roman Catholic theologians. However, the subject matter of dogmatics is as old as the New Testament. The apostolic council held in Jerusalem around 50 AD, led by Peter and James, decided that Gentile Christians were not obligated to observe the ceremonial regulation of the Jews concerning circumcision.[3] The Apostle Paul was insistent on maintaining the "truth of the gospel."[4] The author of 2 Timothy warned that "the time is coming when people will not put up with sound doctrine, but have itching ears . . . and they will turn away from listening to the truth and wander away to myths."[5] The seeds of orthodox Christian teaching were planted by the first generation of Christian evangelists and teachers; they exhibited great passion for true *sophia* (wisdom), *gnosis* (knowledge), and *marturia* (witness).

   2. What conveys Christ!
   3. The account of this council is recorded in Acts 15.
   4. Galatians 2:5
   5. 2 Timothy 2:3–4

INTRODUCTION

The ancient church struggled for its life during the first three centuries of the Christian era. Externally its very survival was threatened by the persecutions decreed by the Roman emperors—most notoriously Nero and Diocletian. Internally its Christ-centered message was challenged by the infiltration of Gnosticism, a sophisticated intellectual amalgamation of the apostolic gospel of the New Testament with pagan mythology and Hellenistic philosophy. Then dogmatics took the form of apologetics, a style of theology written to defend the Christian faith to the outside world. Justin Martyr was an early apologist who used the concepts of Greek philosophy to express the biblical message. Later church fathers, such as Clement and Origen of Alexandria, appropriated the philosophical categories of Plato to express the biblical revelation. But early on the use of philosophy in theology found its severest critic in Tertullian (160–230 AD), of North Africa. He famously asked, "What has Athens to do with Jerusalem or the academy with the church?" His answer was "nothing," a response frequently echoed in the history of theology as well as by critics today concerned to safeguard the purity of the biblical message from philosophical admixtures.

Dogmatics has its closest companion in systematic theology. The difference is chiefly that dogmatics expounds the teachings of the Christian faith straightforwardly in language drawn mostly from the Scriptures and the creeds of the church, whereas systematic theology tends to also use philosophical disciplines, such as epistemology and metaphysics, to construct a system of understanding that encompasses all human experience and knowledge accessible to reason. Augustine used Neoplatonic philosophy, Thomas Aquinas used Aristotle, and what about Martin Luther? Though he was influenced by the nominalist philosophy of William Ockham and actually began his career as a professor of philosophy at the University of Wittenberg, he became disillusioned with philosophy. He turned his attention to the study of theology, earned a Doctor of Theology degree, and from that point on drew his theological inspiration chiefly from the Scriptures. However, Martin Luther's example did not discourage subsequent Protestant theologians from constructing comprehensive systems of theology using philosophy to serve as their handmaiden. The list of philosophers whose ideas influenced post-Reformation theologians is virtually endless—Descartes, Locke, Hume, Leibniz, Lessing, Spinoza, Kant, Fichte, Hegel, Schelling, Heidegger, Sartre, Whitehead, Hartshorne, Wittgenstein, Derrida, Foucault, etc. Who next? That gives rise to the question: has a given

INTRODUCTION

theology been strengthened or enfeebled by its close alliance with whatever philosophy happened to be in vogue at a particular time?

The task of dogmatics is to set boundaries to the beliefs of the Christian community and thus to make clear in any given period what the church believes and confesses as true and what it does not. Since earliest times Christianity has struggled to draw the line between orthodoxy (true teaching) and heresy (false teaching). The Apostles', the Nicene, and the Athanasian Creeds were formulated and adopted by the councils of the church to ward off heresies and to set forth the true doctrines of the Christian faith. The widespread circulation of both Jewish and Gnostic heresies also made it necessary to create the canon of New Testament writings. Many Gospels and epistles circulating in the early Christian communities claimed to be authored by the first apostles; under the guidance of the Holy Spirit only a select few made it into the canon for good. For generations scholars debated which books belonged in the canon and which did not. Luther is famously quoted as saying that the Letter of James scarcely belongs in the canon, and he was equally dubious about the Revelation to John. For all practical purposes all churches treat the canon as closed today, thanks in part to the invention of the printing press.

Dogmatics receives its subject matter from the past, from the Scriptures and the tried and tested creeds and confessions of the church, from what is commonly called the classical Christian tradition or simply the "great tradition." Dogmatics exists for the sake of the church, to teach the faith through catechetical instruction to the laity and to guide its preachers and evangelists in their outreach to the world. Many interrelated topics are dealt with: 1. Most outlines of dogmatics begin with the Holy Scriptures, as does this one, to honor its preeminence over all other testimonies to God's history of revelation and story of salvation. They are the norm that supersedes all other norms in the Christian tradition, creedal or confessional. 2. The next topic in order will focus on God who is the acting subject named in the first verse of the book of Genesis—the God of creation who created the heavens and the earth. This is the same God named in the first verse of the Gospel of John, the Word who was in the beginning with God and who was God, through whom all things came into being, and who became flesh in the person of Jesus. This is the root of the church's doctrine of the Holy Trinity, three co-equal persons, Father, Son, and Holy Spirit. 3. The third topic deals with the knowledge of God and the sources of revelation. What can be known of God through nature and reason—general revelation? And what can be known through the Old and New Testaments that record God's particular revelation through the history of Israel, the ministry of Jesus, and the apostolic community? 4. The fourth topic deals with the first work of God, the creation of the world and the human being in his own image *(imago dei)*. 5. The fifth topic focuses on the fall of humanity into sin and the onset of evil in the world. The question of theodicy is bound to come up, even though we can appeal to no dogmatic consensus. 6. Christology is our sixth topic, treating the person of Jesus Christ. Most of the disputes in the ancient church focused on the question whether he is truly God and truly human. 7. The seventh topic deals with the work of Christ, accomplishing reconciliation and atonement through his death on the cross and resurrection from the grave. 8. The eighth topic is devoted to the Holy Spirit, who proceeds from the Father and the Son, and who applies the gifts of salvation to those who believe. 9. The ninth topic deals with the confession of the one, holy, catholic and apostolic church, despite the fact that the churches we know are badly divided, sinful, parochial, and self-aggrandizing. 10. The tenth topic deals with the holy sacraments, Baptism and the Lord's Supper, the means of grace that mediate Christ *in, with*, and *under* the visible signs of water, bread, and wine. 11. The eleventh topic deals with the Christian responsibility for the world, with the ways faith is active in works of love in pursuit of freedom, peace, and justice for all. 12. The twelfth topic deals with the church's worldwide evangelistic mission, in obedience to Jesus' command to go and tell the gospel to all the nations. 13. The thirteenth topic brings this project of dogmatics to a close, focusing on the future and final end of all things (eschatology).

The topics outlined above—from the alpha of creation to the omega of redemption—are common to the doctrinal traditions (dogmatics) taught by all Christian churches. However, they do not all teach the same things in exactly the same way. It would be fanciful to expect that any single textbook of dogmatics can serve adequately the needs of all church traditions. This book of ecumenical dogmatics is written within the tradition of the reforming movement called "evangelical catholic." Luther did not claim to be a Lutheran. He asked that no one be named after him. His aim was to reform the church he loved, the one that baptized, confirmed, and ordained him, and not to exchange it for another. He maintained continuity with the teachings of the mainstream of the Western Catholic tradition, only convinced of the need to discontinue erroneous medieval developments perceived to be in conflict with Holy Scripture and the creeds of the ancient church. Many Christians in all denominations, including Roman Catholics, now also think of themselves as "evangelical catholics."

Evangelical catholics do not think of themselves as heirs of modern Protestantism, something Karl Barth called a heresy, because of its betrayal of the founding confessions and catechisms of the Reformers (e.g., Luther and Calvin). The Augsburg Confession, the prime confession of Lutheranism, states: "We have introduced nothing, neither in doctrine nor in ceremonies, that is contrary to Scripture or the catholic church." This is why "evangelical catholic" is not an oxymoron, as some have averred. The terms are not contradictory; each contributes something essential to the fullness of the one holy apostolic church. The adjective "evangelical" does not subtract anything from the church catholic.

Luther's vision of the church includes seven marks, which are essential for every church worth its salt, that is, evangelical, catholic, and orthodox. They are: preaching, baptism, holy communion, office of the keys (absolution), the offices of ministry, public worship, and the cross (suffering of believers for the gospel, most notably martyrdom).

These seven marks of the church have been substantially reaffirmed within the modern ecumenical movement. For example, the manifesto of the New Delhi Assembly (1961) of the World Council of Churches states: "We believe that the unity we seek which is both God's will and his gift to the Church is being made visible as all in each place who are baptized into Jesus Christ and confess him as Lord and Savior are brought by the Holy Spirit into one fully committed fellowship, holding the one apostolic faith, preaching the one gospel, breaking the one bread, joining in common prayer, and having a corporate life reaching out in witness and service to all and who at the same time are united with the whole Christian fellowship in all places and all ages in such wise that ministry and members are accepted by all, and that all can act and speak together as occasion requires for the task to which God calls his people."

Some observers have opined that the ecumenical movement has stalled. It has given way to an "ecumenical winter." Much of the original thrill of learning new things has been replaced by a ho-hum feeling of weariness. This may be due largely to unrealistic expectations. The truth is that the modern ecumenical movement is a miracle that only the Holy Spirit of God could have brought about in one or two generations. Amazing consensus has been reached between major church traditions on many—not all—traditional controversial doctrines. The degree of consensus reached between Roman Catholic and Lutheran theologians has been equalled in other bilateral dialogues as well. Traditional articles of faith in dispute between Lutherans and Roman Catholics have been the subject of dialogues at the highest level of authority and competence, by the Lutheran World Federation and the Pontifical Council for Promoting Christian Unity. Among the most important themes are: Scripture and tradition, justification by faith, the saints and Mary, papal primacy and infallibility, and the church and the offices of ministry. The dialogue commissions exhibited no fear in tackling the most intractable issues, producing statements of agreement that have led to a mutual recognition of their unity in Christ, though still indwelling separate institutions and systems of governance. Roman Catholic ecclesiology since Vatican II acknowledges that all Christians are members of the one body of Christ through baptism and faith. They are called "separated brethren" because their communities are not real churches; they lack apostolic succession in the sacrament of orders, an essential mark of the true church. Vatican II called non-Roman communities "ecclesial," a term supposedly inferior to "church." This terminological argument seems to ignore the fact that *ecclesia* is the New Testament word for "church." Consider Matthew 16:18, a favorite passage of Roman Catholic ecclesiology, "upon this rock I will build my *ecclesia*." Non-Roman Christians may rejoice that they are counted as members of the *ecclesia* (church) that Christ founded. Every church in essential continuity with the *ecclesia* that Christ founded is a member of the one, holy, catholic, and apostolic church.

Questions for Discussion

1. How is an "ecumenical dogmatics" intentionally different from one written for a particular denomination, say, a Catholic dogmatics or a Reformed dogmatics?

INTRODUCTION

2. What is the purpose of a church confessing the ancient creeds of the church? Some churches refuse to accept any particular creeds because they believe that creeds divide, whereas Christ unites. What do you think about that?

3. Contrast the "revisionist" and "confessionalist" approaches in constructing Christian theology for today. Reflect on the strengths and weaknesses of each approach.

4. What is the difference between dogmatic theology and apologetic theology?

5. Karl Barth wrote dogmatic theology; Paul Tillich wrote systematic theology. Is that a difference in name only? If not, what is the methodological difference?

6. Some Protestants and some Catholics call themselves "evangelical catholics." What do they mean respectively by doing that? Some say the term is an oxymoron. Do you agree?

7. Name the seven marks of the church according to Martin Luther. Are they all of equal importance? Can a church be a true church if it lacks any of the marks?

1. The Holy Scriptures

The Holy Scriptures of the Old and New Testaments possess unique and incomparable authority in the church because they are the original witnesses to the God of Israel who delivered his revelation in Jesus Christ for the salvation of the world. All the churches acknowledge Holy Scripture as the revealed Word of God inspired by the Holy Spirit. Holy Scripture is foundational for what churches believe and teach in performing their ministry and mission to the world. However, in spite of this common affirmation, the Scriptures have been and continue to be the subject of numerous and still unresolved controversies. Chief among them is the long-standing dispute between the churches of the Reformation and Rome. The Council of Trent (1545–1563) of the Roman Church taught a two-source theory of revelation, passed on down to us partly (*partim*) through Scripture and partly (*partim*) through tradition, both to be honored "with the same sense of devotion and reverence." The Reformation taught that Scripture alone (*sola scriptura*) is the critical norm of God's revealed truth in relation to all later church tradition. The Reformers feared that the Roman *partim-partim* theory would open the door to teachings that lack scriptural support, and they claimed that this is exactly what happened. Late medieval teachings developed that cannot be grounded in the literal historical sense of Scripture, such as those surrounding the indulgence controversy that sparked Luther's criticism. To support their case the Reformers pointed out that the Gnostic heresy in the ancient church appealed to secret traditions not found in Scripture. A stalemate ensued, Protestants waving the slogan "Scripture alone," and Catholics "Scripture and tradition." For Protestants the function of tradition is to interpret Scripture, not to be a supplement. For Catholics Scripture is interpreted to conform to church tradition espoused by its official magisterium. For centuries these two diametrically opposite positions stoked the polemics that kept Protestant and Catholics competing in hostile camps, often disgracefully breaking out in violence and war.

Scripture and Tradition

Thanks to the modern ecumenical movement Lutherans and Catholics engaged in an official dialogue on "Scripture and Tradition."[1] They produced seven points of agreement that go far to soften the sharp differences that prevailed for nearly five centuries.

1. Holy Scripture has preeminent status as the Word of God, committed to writing in an unalterable manner.
2. Before the Old and New Testament existed in written form, the Word of God was carried by tradition.
3. Under the guidance of the Holy Spirit Scripture gives rise to the oral proclamation of the gospel.
4. The preeminent status of Scripture does not exclude the function of a teaching office or the legitimacy of doctrinal traditions that protect and promote the reliance of the faithful on the gospel message of Christ and grace alone (*solus Christus* and *sola gratia*).
5. There are no historically verifiable apostolic traditions that are not attested in some way by Scripture.
6. Not all true doctrine needs to be simply and literally present in the Bible, but may be deduced from it.
7. The teaching of doctrine in the church is never above the Word of God, but must serve that Word and be in conformity with it.

These seven points, as true as they are, do not resolve the difference between the Protestant insistence on "Scripture alone" and the Catholic two-source *partim-partim* theory of Scripture and tradition. The joint statement admits the difference, saying "Lutherans hold that Scripture alone is the ultimate norm by which traditions must be judged. Catholics hold that the decisive norm by which doctrines or traditions are judged is Scripture together with the living apostolic tradition, which is perpetuated in the church through the Holy Spirit."[2] The sticky problem for evangelical catholics is that the phrase, "the living apostolic tradition," is not as innocuous as it sounds, because for Roman Catholics the papal teaching office (magisterium) infallibly determines the content of the apostolic tradition

---

1. Skillrud, Stafford, and Martensen, eds., *Scripture and Tradition*, 21.
2. Skillrud, Stafford, and Martensen, eds., *Scripture and Tradition*, 49–50.

in such a definitive way that no appeal to Scripture may call it into question. After much debate the Second Vatican Council's "Dogmatic Constitution on Revelation" clearly reaffirmed the dogma of papal infallibility that in theory and practice goes against the Scripture principle of the Reformation. This leaves certain dogmas of the Roman Catholic Church that have no support in Holy Scripture immune from any criticism.

Luther's strong emphasis on Holy Scripture as the norm to judge all tradition does not mean that later Lutherans held a low view of its significance for the church's life and governance. After Luther and Melanchthon, Martin Chemnitz was undoubtedly the most important contributor to the formation of Lutheranism. He made it clear that the Scripture principle of their church reforming movement was not meant to foster a revolution that tosses out all church traditions. The Lutheran Reformation, on the contrary, has been accused of being too conservative by radical Protestants, as though it were merely halfway removed from Catholicism. Martin Chemnitz prized church tradition very highly. He stated that there are eight sorts of tradition, only one of which needs correction, even rejection. They are: 1. The oral tradition about Jesus of Nazareth is preserved in the New Testament. Here Scripture is the first deposit of the church's tradition. 2. In church tradition the Scriptures were copied, read, preserved, and handed down from age to age. 3. There are apostolic teachings cited by the church fathers not written down in Scripture. 4. There is the exegetical tradition of church scholars expounding the Scriptures. 5. There is the tradition of evolving church doctrine not literally found in Scripture, but deduced from it. 6. There is the patristic tradition, the writings of the church fathers of the first five centuries. 7. There is the tradition of liturgical rites and ceremonies that come from the ancient church. 8. There are traditions of faith and doctrine not grounded in Scripture that the Council of Trent required be held with the "same devotion and reverence." Such traditions are not acceptable, subject to criticism and reform.

The Authority of Holy Scripture

The post-Reformation conflicts between Protestantism and Catholicism in Europe and around the world brought about a tremendous inflation of their rival claims to authority, the authority of Scripture as the Word of God in Protestant Christianity and the authority of the papal office in Roman

Catholicism. At the time of the Reformation the Lutheran confessional writings, notably the *Book of Concord*, and Philip Melanchthon's 1543 *Loci Communes,* contained no article on Holy Scripture. This was soon remedied by Andreas Osiander (1498–1552), whose theology of the Word of God became a mainstay of Protestant dogmatics. According to Osiander there are three forms of the Word of God: 1. the eternal Word (*Logos*) made flesh in Jesus; 2. the living voice (*viva voce*) of the Word in the preaching of the church; and 3. the written Word in the biblical writings of the prophets and apostles. These are the same three forms of the Word of God that Karl Barth made foundational in his *Church Dogmatics.*

In the period of Protestant Scholasticism (seventeenth century) both Reformed and Lutheran theologians explained the authority of Holy Scripture not primarily with reference to its Christ-centered gospel message, as Luther did, but rather on account of their inspiration by the Holy Spirit. The logic is presumably air-tight. Because the scriptural authors were inspired by the Holy Spirit, everything they wrote must be infallible, free from errors (inerrant), and without contradictions. One Lutheran theologian, Johann Quenstedt (1617–1688), wrote that if a single verse of Scripture were deemed to be in error, the entire authority of the Bible would collapse. Some wag humorously opined that thus for Protestants the Bible became a paper pope.

With the rise of the modern methods of historical research during the Enlightenment all ancient documents were subjected to criticism, including the Bible, to ascertain what really happened. Luther himself engaged in biblical criticism; his canon of criticism was from within the Bible, the very gospel itself. He voiced strong words against anything in the Bible that did not conform to the clear message of Jesus Christ. This is not the sort of biblical criticism applied by many modern practitioners of literary and historical science. The Protestant belief in an infallible, inspired, and inerrant Bible, a book of documents reporting ancient historical events, had to be set aside in favor of an unprejudiced inquiry into history, applying the same techniques and methods used in the scholarly investigation of all other relics and remains of ancient times.

The upshot of the last two centuries of historical scientific criticism has forced theologians to develop a new understanding of the role, relevance, and authority of Holy Scripture that does not fly in the face of the facts available to anyone who reads and understands ancient historical records. The Bible is a book of history, and no faculty of faith or exercise of ecclesiastical authority can exempt it from the methods of historical research and interpretation. However, the application of these methods is never neutral. In the post-Enlightenment tradition of biblical criticism many of its practitioners used them to emancipate religion and morality from the church's faith and doctrine. There is no such thing as exegesis without presuppositions. If the presuppositions are controlled by some ideology, religious or philosophical, other than the church's, the results of biblical exegesis and interpretation will be vastly different. Centuries of biblical scholarship completely divorced from the church's faith and life has proved to be in bondage to a different master, often hostile to the Lordship of Jesus Christ and therefore also to his community.

The modern historical inquiry into the life of Jesus has yielded no consensus among New Testament scholars on a number of questions. "Who was Jesus of Nazareth? What did he say and do? And what happened to him?" The notorious Jesus Seminar, a group of seventy scholars, nicknamed the Sanhedrin, claimed to have come up with sure-fire answers to these questions, but their published findings have been largely rejected or ignored by most reputable biblical scholars. Ever since Albert Schweitzer published his classic monograph *The Quest of the Historical Jesus*, every scholarly attempt to paint a picture of the real historical Jesus has deservedly evoked the judgment, "They found the Jesus they wanted and portrayed him after their own image. They put their own ideology back into the mouth of Jesus." We have witnessed quest after quest of the historical Jesus, from Ernst Renan and David F. Strauss in the nineteenth century to John Dominic Crossan and Marcus Borg in the twentieth century, all of them demonstrating that when pursued by an ideology opposed to the apostolic picture of Jesus as the long-awaited Messiah of the God of Israel, the result is a "so-called historical Jesus," as Martin Kähler so poignantly concluded.[3]

The Interpretation of Scripture

The Bible continues to be a controversial book. Christian churches do not all agree on how to interpret it. Conservatives and fundamentalists

3. Kähler, *The So-Called Historical Jesus and the Historic Biblical Christ*.

continue to assert the authority of Scripture in terms that restore its status prior to the rise of modern historical criticism. In this view Scripture is the church's authority because the Holy Spirit dictated what its human authors were told to write down and the very words to use. Protestant theologians who believe they cannot turn back the clock to a pre-scientific age have favored a concept of biblical authority more in line with Luther's appeal to its Christ-centered gospel message (*was Christ treibt*). To cite a few examples, for Karl Barth the Bible is authoritative because it is the Word of God's self-revelation. For Oscar Cullmann the Bible is authoritative because it is the record of God's history of salvation, whose mid-point is Jesus Christ (*Heilsgechichte*). For Rudolf Bultmann the Bible announces the *kerygma* (message) of Christ and generates an existential response of faith.

Roman Catholic theologians have also accepted the challenge of developing an understanding of Scripture's authority in terms that affirm the modern methods of literary and historical criticism. The Pontifical Biblical Commission produced a document entitled *The Interpretation of the Bible in the Church*.[4] This statement by Catholic biblical scholars is a gift to the whole church. It contains a strong affirmation of two things in tandem: the use of the methods of historical-critical exegesis to ascertain the *content* of Scripture and the role of the community of faith as the appropriate *context* for its interpretation. Reason and faith are both needed to reach a faithful interpretation of the revelation of God attested by the Bible. Hermeneutics is the art of interpreting ancient documents. Every interpretation occurs within a particular context. The significance of the Bible in the living tradition of the church shapes the context presupposed in historical and exegetical interpretation, not subject to any alternative set of presuppositions of whatever provenance. There are no naked facts, only interpreted facts. What we see is always colored by the lens through which we look. That is true for everybody, and the church is no exception.

The Bible still serves the church as its final and binding authority today in matters of faith and doctrine. It does so in the same way it has always served, ever since the apostolic memories were inscribed in the manuscripts the church over time assembled into Holy Scripture. The Bible defines the church's identity and describes its mission in the world. The Bible informs

---

4. The English text is available in *Origins*, CNS Documentary Service, vol. 23, no. 29 (January 6, 1994), 497–524.

the church whom to worship, what to preach, and what sacraments to nourish its spiritual life. Very early in its history the church accepted the Bible as the norm by which to judge what is essential for its entire future life on account of its life-giving message of salvation in Christ. Thus the authority of the Bible derives from the authority of the church's Lord, because it contains the original witnesses to Jesus Christ and the mode of his presence in the power of the Spirit. Thus the ecclesial *context* and the christological *content* together establish the authority of the Bible for evangelical catholics.

All the churches today use the Bible as their chief source for preaching, worship, and for the personal devotion of their members. Every generation produces new translations of the Bible not only to make it more faithful to the original Hebrew and Greek texts, but also to make it easier to read in the everyday language of every nationality and the dialect of every ethnic group. The more traditional churches (Orthodox, Catholic, Anglican, Lutheran) use the pericope system that appoints readings from the Old Testament, Epistles, and Gospels, following the structure of the church year with its special festivals, like Christmas, Easter, Pentecost, etc. The more independent churches tend to be more free-wheeling, opting for readings, hymns, and sermon themes that meet the felt needs of the congregation. The Bible is also the chief document in preparing clergy for their ministry, to guide, support, and shape their preaching and teaching of the laity. When we look to church history we see that the Bible has been the chief impetus to its reformation and the revival of Christian faith and discipleship.

Questions for Discussion

1. Explain the "two source" (*partim-partim*) theory of revelation by the Council of Trent and compare it to the Reformation understanding of "*sola scriptura*."
2. Roman Catholics and Lutherans have engaged in dialogue on "Scripture and Tradition." How significant are their agreements and what remains to be resolved?
3. How important is tradition for Martin Chemnitz? What is his criterion to decide which traditions are acceptable and which are not?

4. Do you think the application of the modern method of historical scientific criticism in biblical interpretation necessarily undermines the authority of Scripture in the church?

5. What is the theological significance of the modern search for the real Jesus of history? What important contribution did Albert Schweitzer make to the enterprise?

6. Explain the meaning of "hermeneutics." What are some of the essential factors to consider in a faithful interpretation of Scripture?

7. What is the importance of the Bible for the church and for each individual Christian?

2. The Holy Trinity

The church of the first five centuries declared that there is one God in three persons, Father, Son, and Holy Spirit. It also confessed that the Trinity is a mystery, that is, totally beyond the capacity of human reason to fathom. The knowledge of the Trinity is based on God's revelation of his being, attributes, and actions in the Holy Scriptures. We can at best try to comprehend the mystery of the triune God by using analogies taken from the sphere of human experience and knowledge. For this reason theologians have used terms to speak of the Trinity not found in Scripture, terms such as *substance, essence, hypostasis, person, nature,* and *accidents*. Church theologians used technical terms drawn from Greek philosophy to defend trinitarian doctrine against alternative teachings not in accord with God's self-revelation according to the Scriptures.

The Reformers, John Calvin and Martin Luther, as well as the Lutheran and Reformed Confessions of the sixteenth century, reaffirmed the traditional doctrine of the Trinity taught by the church fathers and creeds of the ancient church. They confessed that there is one divine essence subsisting in three persons. The confession of God as Father, Son, and Holy Spirit does not mean that there are three Gods, each having his own divine essence, but only one God (*non tres Dii, sed unus Deus*). Furthermore, Father, Son, and Spirit equally coexist in the one divine essence and share equally the divine attributes. No one person is greater or less than the other. Yet, though equal with respect to essence and attributes, the plurality and diversity in God allow for certain real distinctions of personal agency. Thus, the Scriptures speak of the Father begetting the Son, and of the Spirit proceeding from the Father and the Son (*filioque*).[1]

---

1. The original Greek text of the Nicene Creed did not include the *filioque*; the word was added in the Latin text at the Council of Toledo in 589 AD. This has been an ongoing subject of dispute between the Western Catholic and the Eastern Orthodox branches of Christianity.

The creation of the world is ascribed to the Father, redemption to the Son, and sanctification to the Spirit, yet at the same time all the works of the Trinity are undivided (*opera trinitatis indivisa sunt*).

Present-day theologians do not customarily use the categories of the ancient creeds in their construction of the doctrine of the Trinity. Rather than using non-biblical terms such as *essence, substance, nature,* and *accidents*, they prefer to use more biblical concepts, symbols, and metaphors. Neither they nor their readers are well versed in the technical distinctions of Hellenistic metaphysics. Nevertheless, the ancient creeds of the church are still relevant and instructive in that they condemn alternative trinitarian teachings as heresies, that is, as contrary to the self-revelation of God in the Scriptures. St. Augustine's writing *On the Trinity* is an extensive treatise that identifies misguided efforts—some of them still current—to explain the mystery of the triune God in rational terms. Here are some of the leading anti-trinitarian teachings in the history of the church.

Trinitarian Heresies

Monarchianism (*monos* meaning one and *archein* meaning rule) is the teaching that there is only one divine person who rules the universe and reveals himself in history. This is the antecedent source of unitarianism. This view denies any diversity or plurality in God. Then who is Jesus? Though miraculously conceived of the Virgin Mary he was adopted as the Son of God at his baptism. He remained a mere man. Patripassionism is another form of Monarchianism, which teaches that God the Father is the one who became incarnate in Jesus, who suffered and died for the salvation of the world. Sabellius is the best known heresiarch who taught patripassionism. He taught that there are not three distinct persons in God; there is only one person who appears in three different roles or modes of self-manifestation. Hence this theory is also called modalism. It can be made to sound very biblical, inasmuch as the creeds also refer to creation, redemption, and sanctification as the works of the triune God.

Subordinationism is another type of trinitarian error, maintaining that the three persons of the triune God are not equal. Arius (died 336 AD), a priest in Alexandria and the notorious foe of Athanasius (296–373), taught that the second person of the Trinity did not exist from eternity. He said, "There

2. THE HOLY TRINITY

was when he was not." The Word, the Logos, was created by God with the distinction of being "the first born of all creation." Arianism denied the true divinity of Jesus Christ, still a popular teaching in liberal Protestantism dating back to Friedrich Schleiermacher and Adolf von Harnack. The Nicene Creed countered Arianism by confessing that the one Lord Jesus Christ is "true God from true God, begotten not made, consubstantial [of one being] with the Father." It goes without saying that tritheism, the idea that the three persons are three individual gods, so that the Trinity is a community of three gods, is also not in accord with orthodox teaching. The church's confession of the triune God has continued to be challenged and criticized not only by the major world religions other than Christianity but also by modernist and revisionist theologians who still claim to be Christian. The Jewish and Muslim religions are both radically unitarian and accuse Christianity of idolatry, the worship of a being less than God.

The doctrine of the Trinity has not always fared well in modern Protestant theology, all too often reflecting its total rejection by the rationalistic philosophers of the eighteenth century Enlightenment. Immanuel Kant (1724–1804) wrote: "From the doctrine of the Trinity, taken literally, nothing whatsoever can be gained for practical purposes, even if one believed that one comprehended it—and less still if one is conscious that it surpasses all our concepts."[2] Theologians influenced by Kant, most notably Albrecht Ritschl (1822–1889), Wilhelm Herrmann (1846–1922), and Adolf von Harnack (1851–1930), treated the doctrine of the Trinity as dispensable, not in harmony with the teachings of Jesus, and a product of the so-called Hellenization of the gospel. Schleiermacher (1768–1834) relegated his treatment of the Trinity to the Appendix of his dogmatics.[3] Karl Rahner (1904–1984) surveyed the way the Trinity has been handled in modern theology, not only by Protestant but also by Catholic theologians, concluding that the doctrine had become dysfunctional. He wrote: "Christians are in their practical life almost mere monotheists. We must be willing to admit that, should the doctrine of the Trinity have to be dropped as false, the major part of religious literature could well remain virtually unchanged."[4] He further complained, "The Trinity occupies a rather isolated position in the total dogmatic system. To put it crassly . . . when the treatise is concluded,

2. Quoted in Jürgen Moltmann, *The Trinity and the Kingdom*, 6.
3. Schleiermacher, *The Christian Faith*.
4. Rahner, *The Trinity*, 17.

its subject is never brought up again. . . . It is as though this mystery has been revealed for its own sake, and that even after it has been made known to us, it remains, as a reality, locked up within itself. We make statements about it, but as a reality it has nothing to do with us at all."[5]

Renewal of Trinitarian Theology

All that has changed in a remarkable way with the twentieth century renewal of trinitarian theology by Karl Barth. He structured his *Church Dogmatics* on the trinitarian self-revelation of God as Father, Son, and Holy Spirit. Karl Rahner also made a decisive contribution to the renewal of trinitarian thought. Rahner stated that the "immanent Trinity" (the eternal being of God within himself) and the "economic Trinity" (God acting in the history of salvation) are one and the same. Rahner's axiom provides the key to understanding the Trinity, followed by a whole school of trinitarian thinkers from across the ecumenical spectrum. After Karl Barth's massive volumes of trinitarian dogmatics, other important contributors to the renewal of trinitarian theology were Wolfhart Pannenberg and Robert W. Jenson (Lutherans), Walter Kasper and Catherine LaCugna (Roman Catholics), Jürgen Moltmann and Colin Gunton (Reformed), and John Zizioulas and Kallistos Ware (Eastern Orthodox). Together all of them demonstrate that a paradigm shift has occurred in how Christian theology is constructed.

Thomas Kuhn (1922–1996) defined a paradigm as "an entire constellation of beliefs, values, techniques and so on shared by members of a given community."[6] A shift in paradigm occurs when new experience and knowledge call for a change in outlook and methodology. A good example is the paradigm shift from the old Ptolemaic picture of the three-story universe to the Copernican revolution in which the earth and the other planets move around the sun. The trinitarian paradigm says that there is no other God than the one who became human in the crucified and risen Lord Jesus Christ, no other God than the one whose Spirit created the missionary church of the apostles and all in its succession down to the present time. We need not search for a God above and beyond the events that took place in time and space in which God identified himself in the flesh and blood of the man Jesus.

5. Rahner, *The Trinity*, 14.
6. Kuhn, *The Structure of Scientific Revolutions*.

2. THE HOLY TRINITY

The trinitarian paradigm is as old as the New Testament, the Nicene Creed, the church fathers—Irenaeus, Athanasius, and Augustine—as well as the Reformers, Martin Luther and John Calvin. The seeds of trinitarian doctrine were sown when at the beginning of the Christian movement some Jews began to call on the name of Jesus in worship, something that must have seemed blasphemous for monotheists who were instructed not to worship any other God than YHWH. The first Christians worshiped the one God of Israel, whom they praised in worship as the Father of Jesus Christ. Now these first Jewish followers of Jesus prayed prayers of petition and praise that associated Jesus with the holy name of YHWH. Within the worship context of the apostolic community the preaching of the gospel identified this one human being, Jesus of Nazareth, not merely as a good and righteous man, not merely as a prophet whose moral teachings they followed, but as the crucified and risen Lord with whom the God of Israel identified himself in a unique way. He sits at God's right hand and rules with God's own authority.

The Apostle Paul put it succinctly: "God was in Christ reconciling the world to himself."[7] No one in the tradition said it more emphatically than Luther: "True Christian theology does not present God to us in his majesty. . . . Nothing is more dangerous than to stray into heaven with our idle speculations, there to investigate God in his incomprehensible power, wisdom, and majesty. . . . Take hold of God as Scripture instructs you. You must know there is no other God than the Man Jesus Christ. Take hold of him. Cling to him with all your heart, and spurn all speculation about the Divine majesty, for whoever investigates the majesty of God will be consumed by his glory. I know from experience what I am talking about. We must look at no other God than the incarnate and human God."[8] And so Jesus of Nazareth is the person whom God exalted by raising him from the dead, by virtue of which his is "the name that is above every name."[9] As good Jews the earliest Jesus-followers were taught to believe that only God can save, but now because of Jesus they came to believe and confess that "there is salvation in no one else, for there is no other name under heaven given among mortals by which we must be saved."[10] Thus the con-

---

7. 2 Corinthians 5:19.
8. Luther, *Lectures on Galatians 1–4*, 29.
9. Ephesians 1:21.
10. Acts 4:12.

struction of trinitarian faith from the beginning to the present rests on a tripod of history, kerygma, and dogma—the history of Jesus, the kerygma of the apostles, and the dogma of the church. To eliminate any one of the three legs is bound to result in a faith other than Christian.

Trinity and Church

The church's trinitarian confession contains three articles. Modern Christian theology has frequently see-sawed between two kinds of unitarianism. A unitarianism that constructs its doctrine of God exclusively on the first article of the creed leads to radical monotheism or deism. There is also the kind that H. Richard Niebuhr criticized as a "unitarianism of the second article."[11] This can be seen in some brands of conservative Evangelicalism that focus on "Jesus only," replacing a full-throated reference to the triune God. The triune name of God as Father, Son, and Holy Spirit is often conspicuously absent from their preaching, prayers, and praise ditties.

The new affirmation of the Trinity has been not only a matter of intramural interest within the guild of twentieth century dogmatic and systematic theologians; it has also had an ecumenical impact in the drafting of conciliar documents that call the churches to strive toward the goal of visible unity in one faith and in one eucharistic fellowship.[12] Historically churches have been unwilling to be in communion with other churches that do not share the same confession of faith. Trinitarian churches are not in communion with Unitarian churches nor with the Mormon Church that rejects the doctrine of the Trinity. As such they act in the spirit of the Apostle Paul who admonished Galatian Christians that "if anyone proclaims to you a gospel contrary to what you received, let that one be accursed!"[13] Church unity is virtually inconceivable apart from sharing in common the confession of the triune God. According to Ephesians 4:4–6: "There is one body and one Spirit, just as you were called to the one hope of your calling, one Lord, one faith, one baptism, one God and Father of all." The apostolic mission gathered and welcomed people from many nations, cultures, languages, and ethnicities into one communion of faith modeled on the unity of the

11. Niebuhr, "The Doctrine of the Trinity and the Unity of the Church."
12. Cf. *Confessing the One Faith*.
13. Galatians 1:9.

Father, Son, and Holy Spirit.[14] Modeled on the Trinity, the church ideally gives ultimate value to the mutuality of love and service in a communion of equals. That is the ideal, unfortunately not the reality. The church is a communion of saints and sinners at one and the same time (*simul iustus et peccator*), a confession that churches today should have no difficulty to make, given the many scandals reported in the secular press having to do with issues of power, money, and sex.

The ecumenical goal of Christian unity is a worthy one not only for its own sake, but also to give impetus to the missionary mandate of the church. Jesus prayed that his followers "may all be one . . . so that the world may believe."[15] Lesslie Newbigin (1909–1998), British missionary to India, called for "the missionary movement to bind to itself afresh the strong name of the Trinity."[16] He was concerned that the missionary movement would end in failure without an explicitly trinitarian doctrine of God to frame the uniqueness and finality of the gospel itself.[17] He cited in particular the pluralistic theologies of religion that relativize the universal validity of the gospel of Jesus Christ, making it merely one among many equally valid systems of belief.[18] He might have been reading Paul Knitter's book *No Other Name?*, which states, "There are Christian theologians who, in their efforts to understand and dialogue with other religions, are clearly and seriously questioning the finality or definitive normativity of Christ and Christianity. They are still a minority voice within the Christian churches. Yet their voices are growing stronger. A new consciousness within Christianity seems to be forming."[19] In the meantime their voices seem to have become the majority because the world missionary movement that Newbigin espoused has come to a halt in virtually all mainline Protestant denominations. By deconstructing the christological origin of the doctrine of the Trinity, the ascendancy of the pluralistic theology

---

14. St. Cyprian stated the consensus that the church is "a people brought into unity from the unity of the Father, the Son, and the Holy Spirit." Quoted in Kasper, *The God of Jesus Christ*, 247.
15. John 17:21.
16. Newbigin, *Trinitarian Faith and Today's Mission*, 31.
17. Newbigin, *Trinitarian Faith and Today's Mission*, 13, 31.
18. Lesslie Newbigin, "The Enduring Validity of Cross-Cultural Mission."
19. Knitter, *No Other Name?*, 145–46.

of the religions puts an end to the gospel mission of the church, leaving nothing to tell to the nations that they need to know.

The function of the doctrine of the Trinity is to instruct the church on how to discriminate between the truth of the saving gospel of Christ and all its heretical and ideological competitors within and outside the church. Karl Barth warned theologians: "If we have not the confidence . . . to say *damnamus*, then we might as well omit the *credimus*. . . . If the Yes does not in some way contain the No, it will not be the Yes of a confession."[20]

The Holy Spirit is the third member of the Trinity, a person in his own right and equal to the Father and the Son. Yet, the Holy Spirit has had a hard time gaining and keeping equality of status as truly God. There have been binitarians since earliest times who believed that the Holy Spirit is essentially the power emanating from God, with no distinct identity as a separate person within the Trinity. It was through the Spirit that God created all things.[21] Moreover, binitarians observed that Scripture mentions prayer to the Father and the Son but never to the Spirit, and the Holy Spirit is never worshiped as God. Their viewpoint did not prevail in the debates leading up to the Nicene Creed (325 AD), which confesses: "We believe in the Holy Spirit, the Lord, the giver of life, who proceeds from the Father and the Son, who with the Father and the Son is worshiped and glorified, who has spoken through the prophets."

According to the Scriptures the Holy Spirit is the bridge from the Father and the Son to the church and the world. The Evangelist John says: "But the Counselor, the Holy Spirit, whom the Father will send in my name, he will teach you all things, and bring to your remembrance all that I have said to you."[22] And Paul the apostle writes: "So also no one comprehends the thoughts of God except the Spirit of God. Now we have received not the spirit of the world, but the Spirit which is from God, that we might understand the gifts bestowed on us by God. And we impart this in words not taught by human wisdom but taught by the Spirit, interpreting spiritual

---

20. Barth, *Church Dogmatics* I/1, 630, 631.
21. Binitarians could cite Genesis 1:2: "The Spirit of God was moving over the face of the waters."
22. John 14:26.

truths to those who possess the Spirit."[23] These passages make clear that the Spirit is not an impersonal energy but rather a personal divine identity capable of doing things alongside the Father and the Son.

Questions for Discussion

1. Why did the early church modify Hebrew monotheism in speaking of God in a trinitarian way?
2. Name three trinitarian heresies and explain why the Nicene Creed identified them as false teaching of the Christian faith.
3. Modern liberal Protestant theologians have criticized the doctrine of the Trinity. What are some of their criticisms? Do you think they are valid, partly valid, or invalid?
4. What does it mean to call the contemporary renewal of trinitarian theology a "paradigm shift"? What is new about the renewal?
5. What are the historical factors that help to explain why the early Christians called Jesus not only the Son of God, but really God?
6. Some monotheists are unitarians, some binitarians, and some trinitarians. What is their chief point of difference?
7. How important is the trinitarian confession in the ecumenical message and mission in reaching out to the nations with religious majorities other than Christian?

---

23. 1 Corinthians 2:11–13.

3. The Knowledge of God

The Christian confession that God has revealed himself in his covenant with Israel and in the gospel of Jesus Christ according to the Holy Scriptures is held in tandem with St. Paul's affirmation that "ever since the creation of the world God's eternal power and divine nature . . . have been understood and seen through the things he has made."[1] The classical Christian tradition from the church fathers of the first five centuries (e.g., Origen and Augustine), the medieval scholastics (e.g., Bonaventura and Thomas Aquinas), and sixteenth century reformers (e.g., Luther and Calvin) has clearly taught that there are two media of God's revelation, through creation and Scripture. God's revelation through creation ("through the things he has made") has been variously called universal, natural, or general and his revelation through the Holy Scriptures (the Old and New Testaments) has been called particular, supernatural, or special. The significance of this is exemplified by the fact that Christian missionaries and evangelists from ancient times to the present have crossed the frontiers of faith expecting to find a revelatory point of contact for their message of salvation in the name of Jesus. They have not preached the saving gospel of the biblical God into a vacuum, but one replete with religious beliefs, symbols, and experiences that point to some luminous presence or numinous powers beyond themselves.

The Special Revelation of God

The special revelation is the good news (gospel) of what God has done once for all in Jesus Christ, reconciling the world unto himself.[2] This event took place in history some two thousand years ago, ever since dividing chronological time in two eras, BC and AD. However, the gospel is not only a story of what took place in past history, in the life, death, and resurrection

---

1. Romans 1:20.
2. 2 Corinthians 5:19.

3. THE KNOWLEDGE OF GOD

of Jesus of Nazareth; it is also a living word (*viva vox*) by means of which the Holy Spirit works through the church's preaching to apply the benefits of God's grace to believing sinners, liberating them from bondage to the "unholy trinity"[3] of sin, death, and the devil.

The special revelation of God in Jesus Christ is unique because there is only one Jesus Christ as witnessed by his disciples and apostles. The apostolic witness to this person as the Lord and Savior of the world cannot be heard in any other religion. The idea of an "anonymous Christ" present in religions other than Christian such as propounded by some modern pluralistic theologians of religion has no basis in Scripture or in the writings of any religion, and because it has no basis in fact the idea is too fanciful to be of value in the dialogues between the religions. The general or natural revelation of God in non-Christian religions does not communicate the same message that God has revealed in Jesus Christ. The four Gospels tell the story of God's coming in the power and glory of his kingdom in the person of Jesus, in his words and deeds, and above all in the double ending of his life, his death on the cross and resurrection from the tomb. This is the matchless eschatological event, the dawning of the new age that the Hebrew prophets foretold would arrive with the birth of the Messiah.

The special revelation of God in Jesus Christ includes the entire span of the biblical history of salvation that began with the call of Abraham, the election of Israel, the giving of the law of Moses, and the messianic prophecies in the Old Testament. This entire sequence of events is preparation for the gospel (*praeparatio evangelica*) of salvation. It is essential to draw a proper distinction between revelation and salvation. Not all revelation promises salvation. Jesus Christ is not the sole revelation of God; he is the sole Savior of humankind. There is salvation in "no other name."

Given a twofold revelation of God through the law of creation (*lex creationis*) and through the gospel of Christ, it is important to distinguish the two kinds of knowledge corresponding to each. Christians like all other human beings exist in a universal framework of structures inescapably governed by law. We can speak of these as "orders of creation." God has placed all human beings in particular structures of existence common to all, such as sexuality, family, community, work, and government. The

---

3. Martin Luther's expression. Cf. Braaten and Jenson, eds., *Sin, Death, and the Devil.*

law and commandments of the living God are revealed through these common structures of human existence. Luther spoke of the orders of creation—family, state, work—as masks of the hidden God (*larvae Dei*). People do not need to believe and confess Jesus Christ to know through conscience what is right and good by way of the law inscribed in the nature of things. Luther put it this way: "God does not have to have Christians as magistrates; it is not necessary, therefore, that the ruler be a saint; he does not need to be a Christian in order to rule; it is sufficient that he possess reason."[4] Cheating and lying are everywhere recognized as wrong, no matter how common they are in every society.

Law and Gospel

Martin Luther taught that theology is the fine art of drawing the proper distinction between law and gospel, neither separating nor equating them. Law and gospel are two modes of God working his will in the world of human experience and social relations. In Genesis 1–11 Israel wrote a preamble to her covenant history, involving the whole human race, placing Adam before Abraham and Noah before Moses, thus acknowledging that the living God was the Lord of the nations prior to the election of his people Israel. Today, as well, God is active in all realms of life, secular and religious, apart from any contact with the church and the preaching of the gospel. The law is the instrument through which God is working, both through the unwritten law in the nature of things and the written codes of law that seek and promote justice. Law is universal; there is no escape. It reaches and touches all persons, communities, and nations in their actual encounters and relationships, establishing a modicum of order in spite of the prevailing sins of lawlessness and injustice.

Atheists, agnostics, and humanists know the law of the hidden God (*deus absconditus*) through the moral conscience apart from faith and the knowledge of the living God of the Bible. There is no promise of salvation in this kind of revelation through the law of the Creator at work in the world, but without it life would come to a dead halt. God is active anonymously through the law that is universally operative in the structures of the world. God's activity is not dependent on or limited by whether or not people are aware of it or acknowledge it. God carries out his purposes in the world through

---

4. *Martin Luthers Werke, Kritische Gesamtausgabe*, XXVII, 418.

political and economic institutions in a secular world whether people know it or not. There is no sphere of life where God is not active through the law to promote his will to pursue peace and justice. Philosophy may call this natural law, but in theology it is more appropriate to call this the law of the Creator because the living God is present and active through the concrete demands that impinge inescapably on all human beings.

Martin Luther called this the work of "the left hand of God," in distinction from the work of "the right hand of God" carried out through the church's ministry of Word and Sacraments that mediates the hope of salvation and promise of eternal life. The law is the fundamental presupposition of the gospel. Thus God has two ways of working in the world, through the law and the gospel. The law of God encounters every human being through the natural orders of life in society through the medium of conscience, the inner sense of what is right and wrong, just and unjust, good and evil. Even kids on the playground call someone out who is breaking the rules. The law is God's way of calling people out who are breaking his commandments, in that the law can terrify, accuse, condemn, punish, and kill. Theologians have debated whether there are two or three uses of the law. The first use of the law, in any case, is political within the public domain, to order society, to prevent chaos, and to punish crime. The second use of the law is religious, which accuses, condemns, and shows the need for the forgiving grace of the gospel. The gospel is the medicine for the human predicament diagnosed by the law. The law wounds, the gospel heals. Each has a different function in the providence of God. The law tells us what we must do; the gospel tells us what God does. The law is expressed in the imperative mood, the gospel in the indicative. The law demands and threatens; the gospel gives and forgives. Thus the law prepares the way for the hearing of the good news of God's forgiving love and acceptance of sinners in need of divine grace. Those who stipulate a third use of the gospel maintain that everyone who believes and accepts the gospel needs also to hear and heed the law of God, that no one achieves a state of sanctification such that it renders the law irrelevant and useless.

No Other Name

The belief that God has revealed himself in many ways—in the world of nature, history, culture, including the religions—does not detract from the exclusive claim of the New Testament that God's gift of salvation is given to humankind in "no other name under heaven" than the name of Jesus Christ of Nazareth.[5] The claim that "God has many names" is advocated by the pluralistic theologians of religion, who also maintain that all religions are equally salvific.[6] They are free to believe that but there is no support for their hypothesis in the Scriptures or in the mainstream of the Christian tradition. Nevertheless, they have a point. There are in fact many different names for God in the religions of Africa, Asia, Europe, and the Americas that manifest some truth, beauty, and goodness that church theologians and Christian missionaries have acknowledged as revealed by the one God of the Bible. Paul and Barnabas said as much to the Greeks in Lystra, that "God has not left himself without a witness in doing good."[7] Paul also addressed the Athenians in front of the Areopagus, saying "Athenians, I see how extremely religious you are in every way. . . . Indeed, God is not far from each one of us. For 'in him we live, and move, and have our being.'"[8] In this passage Paul is affirming that God is not absent in other religions but "now he commands all people everywhere to repent, because he has fixed a day on which he will have the world judged in righteousness by a man whom he has appointed, and of this he has given assurance to all by raising him from the dead."[9] Revelation? Yes! Salvation? No! That is the gospel truth that has never been rescinded by any Christian authority.

The early Greek and Latin Fathers in the Graeco-Roman world taught that the Divine Logos that became flesh in Jesus was universally present and effectively active in the various religions and philosophies apart from biblical revelation. Justin Martyr used the Stoic concept of the seminal Logos (*Logos spermatikos*) to explain why so much truth and goodness can be found outside of Christianity. The Logos presumably spread seeds of wisdom and morality throughout the world beyond the walls of the church. Whether this Logos-idea coming from Greek metaphysics is today the most useful theological bridge to negotiate the traffic between Christianity and other religions has been criticized because it disconnects the Logos from Jesus,

---

5. Acts 4:12: "There is salvation in no one else, for there is no other name under heaven given among mortals by which we must be saved."

6. Hick, *God Has Many Names*.

7. Acts 14:17.

8. Acts 17:22, 27b–28.

9. Acts 17:30b, 31.

3. THE KNOWLEDGE OF GOD

leading to the questionable notion of a *logos asarkos* (unfleshed Word). This idea was given eminent expression in the natural theology of the medieval scholastics and in the rational religion of the Enlightenment philosophers, leading to speculative theories about God and the world detached from the *Logos ensarkos,* the Word of God incarnate in Jesus of Nazareth. It is possible to be sympathetic to the intention of the Logos Christology because it provides a generous estimate of what God is doing in other religions and it identifies a point of contact for the evangelistic outreach to religions and cultures outside the walls of the church. Ernst Benz, one of the pioneers in promoting interreligious dialogue, has said that despite its good intentions "the traditional Logos theology and its modern versions proves itself to be a theological ell which is too short to measure our modern consciousness of history."[10] To abandon the distinction between a universal Logos outside the flesh (*asarkos*) and a concrete Logos in the flesh (*ensarkos*) does not mean to surrender the validity of the idea of a general revelation of God through religion and morality apart from a special revelation in Scripture and the gospel of Christ. The Apostle Paul's verdict stands, "God has not left himself without a witness."[11] It is the ongoing task of theology to understand that, without necessarily relying on the old idea of a *Logos spermatikos.*

Natural Knowledge of God

With the rise of modern atheism some theologians hark back to the days when philosophy boldly claimed to prove the existence of God. Both Plato and Aristotle believed that there is a God knowable by reason alone. Subsequently Christian philosophers banked on the insights of philosophy to show that it is reasonable to believe in God. St. Anselm of Canterbury constructed an a priori ontological argument to prove that God exists, based on the very definition of God.[12] If God is conceived as the most perfect being, it follows that he must exist. For a being that existed merely as an idea in the mind would not be as perfect as one that existed in reality as well. This argument was rejected by Thomas Aquinas, who offered instead five arguments based on observable contingent entities in the world—hence called cosmological—to demonstrate the existence of God. Every entity in

---

10. Benz, "Ideas for a Theology of the History of Religions," 136.
11. Acts 14:17.
12. The ontological argument for the existence of God was later endorsed by Duns Scotus, René Descartes, and Gottfried Leibniz, but was rejected by Immanuel Kant.

23

the world and all entities in the universe come into existence and are moved by an external cause that is not itself caused. Therefore God exists as the uncaused cause or unmoved mover.

Historically theologians have attended to the philosophical arguments for the existence of God, honoring their belief that philosophy is the handmaid of theology. At the same time they have acknowledged that reason by itself does not provide a clear channel of communication between God and humanity. Moreover, such arguments have proved woefully ineffective in counteracting atheism. The rational arguments for the existence of God are only convincing—if at all—to those who already believe in God on other grounds. Blaise Pascal famously said that faith has its reasons which reason does not understand. Belief in the existence of God is manifestly the presupposition of all real theology. Yet, in the face of modern atheism some modern theologians have thrown in the white towel of surrender. They retrieved Nietzsche's thesis that "God is dead," in order to write theology suitable for the secularized Christianity they celebrated in tune with the *Zeitgeist*. The "death of God" theology that captured the headlines around the middle of the twentieth century is now as dead as a dodo.[13] Ludwig Feuerbach (1804–1872) attempted to welcome atheism into the inner sanctum of Christian theology, quickly refuted by his peers as a failed hypothesis. However, the idea of the "death of God" is not in itself nonsense. It happens to be the gospel according to Good Friday. The man hanging there on the cross was not a mere human being. Long before Nietzsche Luther said he believed in the death of God incarnate, reiterating church dogma that on the cross God experienced suffering and death.[14]

Questions for Discussion

1. Identify the sources of God's revelation according to the Bible and the Christian tradition.
2. What is meant by the "orders of creation," and what are they?
3. How do Christians come to know who God is and what he does?

13. The "Death of God" theologians claimed to be inspired by the prison writings of the Lutheran martyr Dietrich Bonhoeffer, who speculated that religion is obsolete in a secular age. Its chief practitioners were John A. T. Robinson, William Hamilton, Thomas J. J. Altizer, and Paul van Buren.

14. See Moltmann, *The Crucified God*.

4. Why is it important for preachers to draw the right distinction between the law and the gospel of God? What effect does confusing them have on the faith of those who hear? Give some examples.
5. Read Acts 17:16–31. Summarize Paul's message to the Athenians in the middle of the Areopagus. Do you find his sermon convincing?
6. Describe the difference between the *Logos spermatikos* and the *Logos ensarkos*.
7. Do you think it is possible to prove the existence of God? Do you think philosophical arguments for the existence of God are apologetically useful or important for Christian faith? Is there any other way to know that God is real?

4. God the Creator

The first words of Genesis in the Old Testament declare, "In the beginning God created the heavens and the earth."[1] The first three verses of the Gospel of John in the New Testament read: "In the beginning was the Word, and the Word was with God, and the Word was God. He was in the beginning with God; all things were made through him, and without him was not anything made that was made." The juxtaposition of these two passages presents the biblical doctrine of creation in a nutshell, underscores its importance for both the Hebrew and Christian communities, and also makes clear the distinctive difference Christ makes. The account of creation in Genesis is the prelude to the history of God with his people Israel, eventually culminating in the account of redemption in the coming of Christ. In the Bible the God who creates the world is one and the same God who redeems the world. Creation and redemption are inextricably linked.

Creation Out of Nothing

"In the beginning!" The first thing that God did outwardly is to create the world and everything in it. God did this without the cooperation of anything or anyone else. There was no pre-existing material that God molded like putty to make the world. Ontological dualism is rejected, the idea that there are two eternal realities, one spiritual and one material. God created out of his own omnipotence and free will, not from any inherent necessity. Creation is the work of the one true God, with the participation of all three members of the Trinity. God created by speaking the universe into existence. Thereafter, the God of the Bible continued to make things happen by speaking in words that human beings—for example, the prophets—could understand. The world that God created is not divine. Pantheism is rejected; God is not the world and the world is not God. God and

---

1. Genesis 1:1.

4. GOD THE CREATOR

the world are not of one and the same substance. The classic expression of this truth is that God created the world out of nothing (*creatio ex nihilo*). The phrase "out of nothing" does not appear in the canonical Scriptures. However, it first came to early expression in the Vulgate translation of the apocryphal book of Maccabees which says that "God made them out of nothing" (*ex nihilo fecit illa Deus*).

The Genesis account of creation repeats the refrain, "And God saw that it was good." Everything that God created is declared essentially good, including all celestial and earthly beings. So where did evil come from? How did evil enter the world? The Bible does not gloss over the reality of evil. Satan or the Devil is the chief of the evil spirits, the prince of darkness, the enemy and adversary of God and of the goodness of God. Philosophers and theologians have beaten their brains trying to reconcile that God created everything good out of nothing, and yet not everything is good. That is a paradox, and Christian theology has had to live with this seemingly self-contradictory belief. If we believe that God created everything that exists and at the same time believe that evil really does exist, then it logically follows that God created evil. But such a logical conclusion has been condemned as heresy, truly a blasphemy of the Creator (*blasphemia creatoris*).

Theodicy

Theodicy is the discipline of philosophical theology that literally seeks to justify God in view of the belief that an omnipotent loving God created a world deemed to be good but is actually permeated by evil. Etymologically theodicy comes from two Greek words, *theos* (God) and *dike* (justice). The term was used by the German Lutheran philosopher, Gottfried Wilhelm Leibniz (1646–1716), who published a work entitled *Essais de Théodicée sur la bonté de Dieu, la liberté de l'homme et l'origine du mal* to vindicate the goodness of God in face of so much suffering and evil in the world. Evil in the world does not conflict with the goodness of God, properly understood. This view has been called "Leibnizean optimism" because, Leibniz argued, the best of all possible worlds is one endowed by the Creator with attributes of freedom, relationship, and reciprocity, enabling the mutuality of love. The reasoning is that if God willed to create morally responsible free beings, he would have to allow for wrong choices to be made. That is what happened. Eve chose to take a bite of the apple and Adam freely concurred.

They were not automatons. But Leibniz's optimism was sourced by another factor, something he probably gleaned from his study of Luther. As a biblical theologian Luther did not confront the problem of evil in a rational speculative way. Rather, he saw that the Bible tells the story of God active in history to oppose evil forces, and finally in the death and resurrection of Christ God declared victory over sin, death, and the devil. For Leibniz too it is on account of sin that we come to know Christ as Redeemer.[2] The original creation is followed by the new creation in Christ, inspiring hope that in the end God will "reconcile to himself all things, whether on earth or in heaven, making peace by the blood of his cross."[3]

Creationism Versus Evolution

The Christian doctrine of creation has become something of a political football in the contemporary controversy over whether biblical creationism should be taught in public schools as well as the scientific theory of evolution. Those opposed maintain that creationism is a religious belief based on the Bible and therefore does not belong in the science curriculum. The creationists interpret the biblical account of creation in Genesis 1–3 as factual history and reject evolutionary science as atheistic. Confusion abounds on both sides of the debate. Some champions of the theory of evolution have elevated it to quasi-religious dogma. After all, it is a scientific theory and is therefore subject to ongoing research and revision.

Charles Darwin (1809–1882) published the theory of evolution to explain human origins. It was attacked as being anti-Christian, even anti-scientific. After that Henri Bergson's (1859–1941) book *Creative Evolution* and Pierre Teilhard de Chardin's (1881–1955) *Phenomenon of Man* both showed convincingly that the scientific theory of evolution and the Christian doctrine of creation are not incompatible. In 1950 Pope Pius XII wrote an encyclical, *Humani generis*, confirming no intrinsic conflict between the Christian faith and the theory of evolution. The Christian faith affirms that God created all things and that everything that developed thereafter

---

2. In a footnote Werner Elert offered a wonderful comment on Leibniz's theodicy. "Leibniz quotes the ancient hymn: 'O sin of Adam, certainly necessary, which was destroyed through Christ's death! O blessed guilt, which deserved to have a redeemer like this one so great!'" Elert, *The Structure of Lutheranism*, 474.

3. Colossians 1:20.

was initiated under the providence and continuing creativity (*creatio continua*) of God. There is no good theological reason to hold to a literalistic interpretation of the Genesis six-day account of creation as though it is reporting historical facts in the modern sense. What Genesis says is true, that "In the beginning God created all things," however and whenever it started. Creationists are doing immeasurable damage to the church by pitting Christian faith against modern science.

Gnostic Dualism

The biblical theology of creation met its most serious challenge from ancient gnosticism. Three church fathers—Irenaeus, Tertullian, and Hippolytus—wrote treatises against the dualistic heresy that taught that the God who created the world is other than the God who redeemed the world. The anti-gnostic fathers responded, No, there are not two Gods. The Redeemer and the Creator are one and the same God. The dualistic view had the advantage of being able to explain the origin of evil in a rational way. This dualistic scheme separated the Old and New Testaments. The Old Testament God, the gnostics said, is the God of the Jews who created this evil world—the inexhaustible source of perennial anti-Semitism.[4] This blasphemous teaching had a tremendous impact on the attitude of the "Nazi Christians" toward the Jews and its contribution to the Holocaust. The gnostic rejection of the Old Testament also meant the rejection of the law, resulting in the heresy of antinomianism (*antinomos*). They believed that since they had the gospel, they had no need of the law; since they had Christ, they had no need of Moses.

Gnostic dualism also separated the created body from the soul. Carpocrates was an early gnostic heretic who defined the soul in radical distinction

---

4. Marcion was a second century gnostic who wrote a book to prove that the New Testament gospel and the Old Testament contradict each other. The God of the Jews and the God of the Christians are opposed to each other. Some German Christian theologians revived this old heresy of Marcion in their campaign against Jews. Adolf von Harnack's book on Marcion prepared the way. He wrote, "The rejection of the Old Testament in the second century was an error which the great church rightly opposed; holding on to it in the sixteenth century was a destiny which the Reformation was not able to escape; but for Protestantism to preserve it since the nineteenth century as a canonical document is the result of religious and ecclesiastical paralysis." Quoted from Kraus, *Geschichte Der historisch-kritischen Erforschung des Alten Testaments*, 351.

from the body, the one being spiritual and infinite, the other material and finite. Carpocratians cultivated the higher spiritual values of the soul, and devalued the physical needs of the body. This body-soul dualism is the source of docetism (from the Greek word, *dokeo*, meaning it seems or appears), the belief that Jesus only appeared to have a human body, and that his physical suffering was not real.

The Christian doctrine of creation is not only of dogmatic significance, teaching the proper way to think about the world in relation to its Creator. It also has ethical significance, committing Christians to a certain way of life and behavior. Christian faith is holistic, expecting every doctrine to have a corresponding ethical dimension. Faith seeks understanding, to be sure, but not without works of obedience to the will of God. In the present situation the ethical challenge is to draw out the implications from the biblical Christian concept of the psychosomatic unity of the human being. The gnostic influence has had the effect of giving priority to matters of the soul at the expense of the body. Platonism taught the immortality of the soul; Christianity taught the resurrection of the body. Christian ministers were told that they were in the business of "saving souls," while leaving the body to other specialists, implying that the body is the inferior part of the person.

Ethics of the Body

The situation has in general changed for the better with the rise of somatic thinking in both philosophy and theology. The combined influence of innovators like Charles Darwin, Ludwig Feuerbach, Karl Marx, Friedrich Nietzsche, and Sigmund Freud upgraded the importance of the physical body in the definition of being human. Twentieth-century theologians such as Karl Barth, Oscar Cullmann, Rudolf Bultmann, Paul Tillich, and Wolfhart Pannenberg all gave due emphasis to the body in answer to the question, "What is Man?" The encounter with God takes place in the body or not at all. A person is nobody without a body. Theology and biology both deal with the same bodily reality. A host of auxiliary scientific studies remind theology to take its own body language seriously. Somatopsychic approaches to healing, bioenergetics, ecology, the organic revolution, and the science of nutrition all invite theologians to remember that Christianity is an incarnational religion. "The Word became flesh."[5] John A. T. Robinson wrote in his book

5. John 1:14.

on the apostle Paul's idea of the body, "One could say without exaggeration that the concept of the body forms the keystone of Paul's theology."[6] Yet, the practice of the Christian faith at the parish level still has a long way to go to overcome the schizoid condition that gnosticism caused by pitting soul against body and spirit against nature. Paul Tournier complains that "all the churches speak of incarnation, but they generally suggest a contempt for the body, as if the spirit had debased itself instead of fulfilled itself in this wonderful venture that God has willed. We find in all our patients, especially in our pious patients, a certain contempt for the body."[7]

Even modern non-Christian philosophers join in the recovery of the somatic essence of human personhood. Ludwig Wittgenstein states that "the human body is the best picture of the human soul."[8] Jean-Paul Sartre says that "I am my body to the extent that I am."[9] These are secular echoes of St. Paul's statement, "You glorify God in your body."[10] This idea counters the gnostic idea that the body is the source of evil. No, the body is good; God created it along with the whole material world. What a contrast to the teaching of the Neoplatonist philosopher, Plotinus (205–270 AD), who remarked, "The true philosopher is entirely concerned with the soul and not the body. He would like, as far as he can, to get away from the body . . . to dissever the soul from the communion with the body."[11] This idea fed into monastic asceticism that denigrated the body because it is made of matter, the source of evil in this world. Archbishop William Temple, in contrast, could declare, "Christianity is the most materialistic of all religions." Biblical religion asserts that there is nothing the matter with matter; God created it and saw that it was good.

Ludwig Feuerbach (1804–1872) was a vigorous critic of idealist philosophy, because its lofty ideas led to the devaluation of the body. He coined the phrase, "You are what you eat."[12] A Christian theology of the body is concerned about the earth and the food it yields, because the earth provides the essential

6. Robinson, *The Body*, 5.

7. Tournier, Preface, 16.

8. Wittgenstein, *Philosophical Investigations*, part IV, section 178.

9. Sartre, "The Body," 233.

10. 1 Corinthians 6:20.

11. Owen, *Body and Soul*, 39.

12. "*Man ist was er isst!*"

nutritional elements for the building of animal and human bodies. The ecology movement is an expression of the Christian concern for the earthly residence of humanity. It is not only insane but sinful to plunder the environment in which we humans live in natural continuity with the earth. If the body is the very stuff of the earth, then soil erosion cannot be a matter of indifference. Similarly, Christians should lead the ecological campaigns for clean air and water. Christians should also be decidedly on the side of those who act ethically in earnest about such concerns as organic and natural foods, holistic medicine, global warming, world peace, and the like.

Questions for Discussion

1. Why is the Christian doctrine of creation "out of nothing" opposed to pantheism?
2. The book of Genesis says that everything that God created is "good." If so, where did evil come from?
3. Define theodicy and explain why it poses such a difficult theological problem. What is your response to the saying, "Why do bad things happen to good people"? Or, "Why do good things happen to bad people"?
4. How would you counsel public school boards that have to decide whether to require the teaching of biblical creationism alongside the teaching of the scientific theory of evolution in the curriculum?
5. What are the chief Christian theological objections to "gnostic dualism"?
6. The Gospel of John 1:14 states, "The Word became flesh." What significance does this assertion have for how Christians should value and treat their bodies?
7. What are the pros and cons for the idea of "antinomianism"?

5. Sin, Death, and the Devil

In this chapter we will deal with the human predicament from a biblical theological point of view under the rubric, "Sin, Death, and the Devil." The human situation can also be made the focus of psychological and sociological studies, among others, which certainly provide valuable auxiliary insights. However, to consider the human condition from a theological perspective means to be informed by the biblical revelation of the God-human relationship as received, understood, and interpreted in the mainstream of the classical Christian tradition, including decisive inputs from the patristic, medieval, reformational, and modern ecumenical periods.

The Nature and Effects of Sin

The Bible contains many words for sin and the effects of sin. In the Old Testament sin is any deviation from what God wills is right and good for human beings, and such failure may be directed against God as well as against other human beings. Transgression against the laws and commandments of God is tantamount to rebellion. Such willful disobedience is defiance of God's word, as the story of the sin of Adam and Eve illustrates. Sin results in guilt and punishment as they were banished from the garden of Eden.

The list of words for sin is long, including pride, obstinacy, uncleanness, backsliding, deceit, etc. All the sins taken together add up to intense personal alienation from a personal God. Isaiah reports that he saw the Lord sitting upon a throne; a voice called out, "Holy, holy, holy is the Lord of hosts; the whole earth is full of his glory." Then Isaiah cried out, "Woe is me! For I am lost; for I am a man of unclean lips, and I dwell in the midst of a people of unclean lips; for my eyes have seen the King, the Lord of hosts."[1] He perceives himself as a sinner in the presence of a holy God. This makes

---

1. Isaiah 6:5.

clear that sin is a theological concept; it makes sense only *coram deo*, in relation to God. In 1973 Karl Menninger, a psychiatrist, published a book with the title *Whatever Became of Sin?*, in which he argued that the loss of sin-consciousness is due to a dimming of God-consciousness. That is exactly right. Sin is not merely a blunder, an error, a mishit, a trivial matter. The Bible takes sin with utmost seriousness because it is an offense against God. It arises from a deep corruption of the heart, the seat of personhood. And the Lord said, "This people draw near with their mouth and honor me with their lips, while their hearts are far from me."[2] Jeremiah writes, "Thus says the LORD: 'Cursed is the man who trusts in man and makes flesh his arm, whose heart turns away from the LORD. . . . The heart is deceitful above all things, and desperately corrupt; who can understand it?'"[3]

Isaiah and Jeremiah were talking about Israel, the people chosen by the Lord, who continually rebelled against God and chose to go their own way. Because they were the people of the covenant, their sin is all the more serious because they should have known and done better. But the severity of prophetic judgment was expanded to include everyone, all the nations, reaching into every thought, word, and deed. Sin is universal. The Psalmist minces no words: "The fool says in his heart, 'There is no God.' They are corrupt, they do abominable deeds, there is none that does good. . . . They have all gone astray, they are all corrupt; there is none that does good, no, not one."[4] And they were that way from the beginning—"from the womb, from their birth."[5] The Psalmist is here expressing what later theology called the doctrine of original sin. All humans since the first pair have been sinful from head to toe, inside and out, from before they were born to the day of their death.

Perhaps this condition of universal sinfulness is an inescapable tragic fate for which humans bear no responsibility. A carnivorous animal can hardly be held responsible for eating its prey. But not so for the Hebrew writers. They left no doubt that sin is a perversion of human freedom. God holds all people accountable for their actions. But that is only half the story. The other half is that God offers a plan to remedy the situation, the offer of grace

2. Isaiah 29:13.
3. Jeremiah 17:5 and 9.
4. Psalm 14:1 and 3.
5. Psalm 58:3.

needed for sinners to repent and mend their ways. Ezekiel 33:11 reads: "As I live, says the Lord God, I have no pleasure in the death of the wicked, but that the wicked turn from his way and live; turn back, turn back from your evil ways; for why will you die, O house of Israel?"[6] God calls upon all people, Hebrews and Gentiles, to quit their wrongdoing, which presupposes responsibility. The idea of corporate inherited sin is also found in the Old Testament, the idea that punishment for the iniquity of the fathers will be visited upon their children. "The Lord . . .will by no means clear the guilty, visiting the iniquity of fathers upon children, upon the third and upon the fourth generation."[7]

It is remarkable that the Old Testament writers do not spare the reputation of those they regard as most worthy and righteous, such as Noah, Abraham, Moses, and David. Noah became drunk with wine and lay naked in his tent.[8] Abraham, to save his skin, surrendered his beautiful wife Sarai to be Pharaoh's concubine.[9] David schemed to have Uriah, his army general, killed in battle so he could take Uriah's wife Bathsheba to be his own wife and, it says, "the thing that David had done displeased the Lord."[10] The prophets held the covenant people accountable for their sins, and even announced that the Lord will use Israel's enemies to execute his judgment. The Babylonian captivity is punishment for Israel's sin. In the eyes of the prophets Israel's predicament is not hopeless. They are called upon to repent and to seek forgiveness. Psalm 130 says it clearly:

> "Out of the depths I cry to thee, O Lord! Lord, hear my voice!
>
> Let thy ears be attentive to the voice of my supplications!
>
> If thou, O Lord, shouldest mark iniquities, Lord, who could stand?
>
> But there is forgiveness with thee, that thou mayest be found. . . .
>
> O Israel, hope in the Lord! For with the Lord there is steadfast love,
>
> > and with him is plenteous redemption,
>
> And he will redeem Israel from all his iniquities.

6. Ezekiel 33:11.
7. Numbers 14:18; Exodus 20:5.
8. Genesis 9:21.
9. Genesis 12:10–16.
10. 2 Samuel 11:27b.

Hundreds of years separated the last book of the Old Testament and the first book of the New Testament—the so-called inter-testamental period. In the writings of this period—the pseudepigrapha—sin as estrangement from God continued to be a concern, but more and more the conception of sin became legalistic, breaking the letter of the law. The line was drawn between the righteous, those who observed the law, and sinners, those who were willful transgressors of the law. It was during this period too that apocalyptic speculations about angels and demons soared. The ground was being prepared for the strains of dualism, probably influenced by Iranian Zoroastrianism, that appeared in the New Testament as conflict between two cosmic powers in the world, experienced in human beings as the struggle between flesh and spirit. New Testament scholarship has become better informed about this New Testament background with the discovery of the Dead Sea Scrolls (1947–56) belonging to the Qumran Community, which practiced extreme asceticism, ritual cleansing, and food taboos.

New Testament Concepts of Sin

The Old Testament hamartiology (doctrine of sin) provided the words and concepts assumed by the New Testament, with the one major difference that the latter are closely linked to the advent of Jesus Christ. The New Testament is chiefly preoccupied with sin in the light of Christ's victory over its deadly effects. Sin's power is great, but Christ's is greater. That is the assurance of the gospel preached. Whereas the Old Testament used Hebrew words for sin, the New Testament used words from classical Greek. The New Testament has many words for sin, each one offering a somewhat different picture of sin and its effect. The most common are as follows.

> *Hamartia* is the most common Greek word for sin, meaning "missing the mark."
>
> *Hettema* is a failure to attain the fullness of what God expects.
>
> *Paraptoma* is falling down when one should have stood.
>
> *Agnoema* is a state of not knowing, inexcusable ignorance.
>
> *Parakoe* is failure to listen and give heed to God's word.
>
> *Parabasis* is to transgress, to cross the line on purpose.
>
> *Anomia* is lawlessness, breaking the law of God.

5. SIN, DEATH, AND THE DEVIL

Asebeia literally means "no worship," godlessness, not honoring God.

Adikia means injustice, not doing what is right.

For the New Testament sin is still defined in relation to the law, but because of Jesus' encounter with the Pharisees and Paul's mission to the Gentiles the scrupulous legalistic attitude characteristic of Judaism was denounced. Jesus condemned the Pharisees as hypocrites, as white-washed sepulchers. He said, "Sabbath was made for man, not man for the Sabbath."[11] Both Jesus and Paul declared that love is the fulfillment of the law. Yet, although both of them observed the law, they counted that as insufficient. Of all the New Testament writers, Paul's theology of sin is the most profound and complex. He personifies sin as an evil power that enslaves human beings, setting sinners in opposition to the law and to God. He depicts the ongoing conflict of Spirit against flesh, of light against darkness, of the new against the old, of Christ versus Adam. Christ is the only effective solution to the problem of sin. That is his mission in the world. "He will save his people from their sins."[12] Jesus is the "Lamb of God who takes away the sin of the world."[13]

The Bible is the primary but not the only source for two millennia of Christian reflection on the nature of sin, its origin and effects. Human experience is the other main source, reflected in the lives of the saints and their personal confessions. The *Confessions* of St. Augustine, Bishop of Hippo, for example, is one such source. Dogmatics has thematized the long tradition on Christian teaching on sin by certain rubrics, which we will follow here.

Original and Hereditary Sin

What is original sin? Genesis 3 tells the dramatic story of Adam and Eve being tempted by the serpent to disobey the Lord God's command not to eat of the fruit of the tree of the knowledge of good and evil, accompanied by the threat that failure to obey would result in death. The consequences of their disobedience were dire. They would experience shame for their nakedness, Eve pain in childbearing, Adam having to labor by the sweat of his brow, and both expulsion from paradise to a life of struggle and

---

11. Mark 2:27.
12. Matthew 1:21.
13. John 1:29.

suffering, ending in death east of Eden. The revelatory truth of this ancient story about Adam and Eve does not depend on taking every jot or tittle as literal historical fact. Historical or not, it has served ecumenical orthodox Christianity as its chief source of the doctrine of original sin.[14] The chief point of this doctrine is to affirm that all human beings, even cute little babies, are born with a sinful inclination. This means that all persons from birth lack true fear, love, and trust in God. In their natural state humans lack the ability to generate the love of God and their fellow human beings. St. Augustine was the first church father to spell this out. The medieval scholastic theologian, Thomas Aquinas, followed him and so did the Reformers, Martin Luther and John Calvin, centuries later. In modern theology Reformed theologians Karl Barth and Emil Brunner, as well as Lutheran theologians Edmund Schlink and Wohlfart Pannenberg, brought fresh thinking to bear on the doctrine, but none more so than the American theologian, Reinhold Niebuhr, in his classic, *The Nature and Destiny of Man*. All of these modern theologians recast the doctrine of sin with an open-eyed acceptance of the modern scientific theory of evolution, without losing any of its doctrinal significance.

Is it really true that human beings are born in a state of original righteousness and have no need of salvation or of a savior? Is it really true that humans can become righteous and pleasing to God in all things by exercising their own free will? Is it really true that humans can love God and keep his commandments by their own innate powers? Just to ask these questions makes those who answer them in the affirmative appear ludicrous. Reinhold Niebuhr is often quoted as having said that the doctrine of original sin is the only empirically verifiable doctrine of the Christian faith. Who can deny that we are all complicit in the evil that abounds in the world? Ingrained sinfulness is everywhere enacted in daily life—in selfish deeds, violence, injustice, lies, and in greed built into every economic system. The Ten Commandments—true today as ever—would not have been published if they did not resonate with the universal human condition. Genesis says that God created man in his own image. The reason that human beings do not act in accordance with their Creator's image is that sin lies deeply

---

14. By ecumenical orthodox Christianity I an alleging that there are no important confessional differences on the doctrine of original sin between the Roman Catholic Church and the Churches of the Reformation (Calvinist and Lutheran).

5. SIN, DEATH, AND THE DEVIL

embedded in the human soul. We can speculate on how or when that came about, but this is the way things are now.

What is concupiscence? Augustine used this heavy word to explain an aspect of original sin that people experience in every age. Preachers are smart not to use that word, because there is an easier word for the same thing—lust. In his *Confessions* Augustine offered lurid details of his insatiable desire for sexual exploits. Concupiscence is lust for carnal things, not limited to sex, of course. By extension it can refer to aggressive desire of material things to gratify and glorify the self, in lieu of loving God above all things. Thus, original sin expresses itself against the first table of the Law (the first three commandments) as well as the second table (commandments four through ten).

The church's teaching on original sin has been challenged on two fronts, on the optimistic side by Pelagianism[15] and on the pessimistic side by Manichaeanism.[16] Pelagius taught that even after the fall human nature remains uncorrupted in spiritual matters, so that human beings by their own free will are able not to sin (*posse non peccare*). To be sure, Pelagius held that Adam set a bad example, but his sin is his alone, not something his descendants inherit. Human beings are all born in a state of innocence, and like Adam and Eve are free to do good and obey the commandments of God. But, alas, when they follow Adam's bad example, that causes the kind of problem the New Testament message of Christ can remedy. So Pelagians are Christians; they happen to be heretics in the judgment of church teaching ever since Augustine.

Pelagian and Manichaean Heresies

Luther was an Augustinian monk who probably surpassed even Augustine in the severity of his judgment against the Pelagian heresy. Luther was equally allergic to the widely prevalent semi-Pelagian teaching among

---

15. Pelagius was a British monk (ca. 360–420), who taught in Rome and vigorously opposed St. Augustine on the nature of sin.
16. Manichaeans were adherents of a religion founded by Manes in the third century, a syncretistic system of Zoroastrianism, Gnosticism, and Buddhism, dualistic in its teaching, with two opposing gods, one good and one evil, light versus darkness, spirit versus matter.

some medieval scholastic theologians that people are not so corrupt by nature and in bondage to sin that if they do the best they can God will be gracious to them.[17] In modern popular jargon, it means, "If I scratch his back, he will scratch my back." Pelagianism has never died out in popular Christianity. In the Reformed tradition it surfaced with Arminianism, associated with the teaching of the Dutch theologian Jacob Arminius (1560–1609), who contradicted the Calvinist doctrines of total depravity, unconditional election, limited atonement, irresistible grace, preservation of the saints (somewhat humorously referred to by the acronym TULIP). In opposition he taught that even after the fall human beings possess free will, with the ability to accept or reject God's grace and offer of salvation. God's election is conditional, dependent on his foreknowledge of how persons would respond. Thus the sinner's choice of Christ, not God's choice of the sinner, is the ultimate cause of salvation. God did not predestine some to be saved and some to be damned. God wants all to be saved, and leaves it up to each individual to choose one way or another. God's grace is resistible; hence the Calvinist belief, "once saved, always saved," is rejected. In his magisterial work, *Creeds of Christendom*, Philip Schaff described Arminianism as "semi-Pelagianism."

Lutheranism suffered a similar fate in seventeenth century German Pietism initiated by Philipp Jacob Spener (1635–1705) and August Hermann Francke (1663–1727), a movement that spread especially to Scandinavia. They emphasized Bible reading, prayer meetings, personal repentance and conversion, lay leadership, while being critical of the so-called "dead orthodoxy" of official Lutheranism. Luther's favorite book, *The Bondage of the Will*, was replaced by a semi-Pelagian affirmation of the role of free will in salvation. The Lutheran *Formula of Concord* taught that the human will is not free, is at enmity with God, and needs to be converted by the grace and power of the Holy Spirit. The Holy Spirit works through the means of grace, the preaching of God's Word that generates the response of faith. The *Formula* rejected the teaching that humans by their own powers have the understanding and ability to accept or reject God's gracious offer of

---

17. Examples of such late medieval scholastic theologians were John Duns Scotus and Gabriel Biel, whose writings Luther studied and knew very well. In particular he objected to the medieval counsel, *"facere quod in se est."* (Translation: "To do what is in one.") If human beings do as much as is in their power, then God will surely give grace to them.

5. SIN, DEATH, AND THE DEVIL

salvation through the preaching of the gospel. Jesus said to his disciples, "You did not choose me, but I chose you."[18]

Manichaeanism is exactly the opposite of Pelagianism, rejected by Augustine because it taught that an evil God created humans essentially sinful by nature. Adam and Eve were sinners from the beginning; there is no such thing as "the fall," because creation itself is the fall into a dark sinful, material world. Augustine countered, "Being as being is good."[19] After each day of creation Genesis iterated, "And God saw that it was good." The Manichaeans said, No, the very substance of the human being is from its very origin nothing but sin.

Manichaeanism has had its successors in the history of philosophy and religion. Also known as Gnosticism, the Manichaean dualistic scheme was taught by a medieval sect known as Catharism or Albigensianism in southern France and by the Bogomils in Bulgaria. As a reaction to the perceived worldliness of the Roman Church and especially its clergy, Albigensianism rejected the material world because it was created inherently evil, and that includes the physical body. The gnostic or semi-gnostic elements continued to survive in post-Reformation Christianity in various types of philosophy and religious sects, as well as in modern liberal Protestantism.[20] Antinomianism (against the law) is a semi-gnostic idea condemned by both the Lutheran and Calvinist confessional statements. Luther himself tangled with those he called "enthusiasts" (*Schwärmer*), who like the gnostics claimed they derived their religious knowledge directly from the Holy Spirit. Luther said they had swallowed the Holy Spirit "feathers and all." The spiritualists of yesterday and today claim to be directly enlightened by the Spirit apart from the written and preached Word (*verbum externum*), thus leading away from Christ and his church. One example among many is the religious philosophy of Mary Baker Eddy (1821–1910), founder of the Christian Science Church. German historian Ferdinand Christian Baur showed how gnosticism seeped into the thought categories of

---

18. John 15:16b.
19. *Esse qua esse bonum est.*
20. The following sources discuss the modern resurgence of gnosticism: Smoley, *Forbidden Faith*; Hoeller, *Gnosticism*; Lee, *Against the Protestant Gnostics*; and O'Regan, *Gnostic Return in Modernity*.

German Idealism and Romanticism.[21] His thesis was followed up by Eric Voegelin, professor of political science at the University of Vienna in the 1930s, who demonstrated the connection between ancient gnosticism and such modern movements as Freudianism, Existentialism, Communism, and National Socialism.[22]

Overwhelming doctrinal consensus prevails between major church bodies that the classical Christian doctrine of sin based on scriptural revelation always steers between the Scylla of Pelagian cosmic optimism and the Charybdis of Manichaean cosmic pessimism, with plenty of room for minor non-church dividing differences in between.

"For the wages of sin is death, but the free gift of God is eternal life in Christ Jesus our Lord."[23] This chapter is dealing with the human condition from a theological perspective under the rubric of sin, death, and the devil. Much more could be said about sin, its nature and effects. The topic is inexhaustible. The Christian dogmatic tradition, taking its cue from the New Testament, has always dealt with the human condition, not for its own sake, but always in light of the gospel of Christ. On account of Christ the gospel promises forgiveness for sin, resurrection from death, and victory over the Devil.

The Destiny of Death

St. Augustine said it well: "Everything is uncertain, with the sole exception of death."[24] We do not know when we will die, but we do know it is inescapable. The gospel tells believers in Christ to anticipate their death in light of his resurrection from the grave. Without faith in the victory of Christ, we are no match for the most powerful enemy in the world. The Apostle Paul said as much: "The last enemy to be destroyed is death."[25] Simone de Beauvoir, one of the French existentialists almost as famous as her husband, Jean-Paul Sartre, wrote about the death of her mother in her book, *A Very Easy Death*. She cared for her mother during the progressive stages

21. This is the thesis of a book by Ferdinand Christian Baur, *Die christliche Gnosis*.
22. Voegelin, *Science, Politics, and Gnosticism*. See also Jonas, *The Gnostic Religion*.
23. Romans 6:23.
24. *Incerta omnia, sola mors certa*.
25. 1 Corinthians 15:26.

of dying. She told how death shook her own confidence in life and how she became totally revolted. Sartre had a word for it in the title of his play, *Nausea*! Simone could not talk to her mother about her inevitable death. She had to go on kidding her that her illness could be cured and that she would soon get better. She did not know what to say to her mother to comfort her. She lived only in the awareness that death involves sinking into absolute nothingness, with no hope or prospect of life beyond. No Easter, to tell a different story. As an existentialist she had literally nothing to look forward to except anxiety, despair, boredom, and futility.

Perhaps the more common approach to death in our time is to deny it. Ernest Becker wrote a book entitled *The Denial of Death*. If we cannot face dying in light of Easter's victory, we may, like many of our contemporaries, try to cover it up through the pursuit of intoxicating pleasure—drugs, alcohol, sex, or whatever will numb the nerves of our awareness that fatality awaits. Or we may beautify the deadliness of death with flowers, cosmetics, and music. Americans spend billions covering up the stark reality of death, making the dead look as life-like as possible. We speak in euphemisms about death, like "passing away," "going home," "falling asleep." And on the day of Easter, while some are chanting "He is risen!" others seem satisfied with eggs, bunnies, and lilies. Some pretend they have no fear of death and instead live by the Epicurean dictum, "Eat, drink, and be merry, for tomorrow we die."

Because everyone in every society and in every age knows that death is the definitive end of life, smart people—scientists and philosophers—have proposed ways to deal with it. Walter Kaufman, writing from the perspective of scientific naturalism, the most common way in our postmodern secular culture, voices criticism of the biblical-Christian view that death is the wages of sin, and alleges that death is merely the necessary end of every creature within the ecosystem of nature. Everything that is born and lives must also die and be recycled into the earth, later perhaps to become food for other creatures. Human life is no exception to this natural process. Kaufman is telling the truth, something everybody knows for certain. But is that all there is to it? Why then do people flee from their death? He blames Christianity for inculcating the dread of death.[26] This nonsense is

---

26. Kaufman, "Existentialism and Death."

contradicted by the fact that the fear of death prevailed before the Christian Era and is present in non-Christian societies.

Sigmund Freud wrote that "At bottom, nobody believes in his own death. Or, and this is the same: In his unconsciousness, everyone of us is convinced of his immortality."[27] The ancient Greek philosophers—Socrates, Plato, and Aristotle—would have agreed with that sentiment. In his *Apology* Plato depicts Socrates facing death with the assurance, "To die is gain." Death is a journey to a better place. In his final address to the Athenians Socrates spoke of death as a liberation of the soul. Death is viewed as greeting mortals with a friendly face. Plato taught the doctrine of the immortality of the soul. When a person dies, only the physical body dies. The soul—the spiritual essence of a person—does not die. Ezekiel 18:4 and 20 states without qualification, "The soul that sins dies." Not just the outer garment, not only the bag of bones, the person at the core of his or her being is subject to death. Not so for Plato and the Greek philosophers. The soul is guaranteed a destiny beyond the reach of the Grim Reaper.

The Platonic idea of immortality is not a specifically Christian answer to the question of hope for a death-transcending future. Nevertheless, the Greek fathers in the ancient church, influenced by Plato's anthropology, introduced the idea of immortality into the Christian tradition, but not without modifications. They did not deny that death is the wages of sin. To overcome death it is necessary to share in the divine life, by eating the divine food. A person must receive the medicine of immortality, the "*pharmakon athanasius*." This is a gift a person receives at the Lord's Supper, the sacred meal that communicates immortality, by eating the immortal body of the risen Lord and drinking his blood. This is the power of immortality that alone can overcome the death-ridden finitude of human beings. Thus the two images, immortality and resurrection, merged, and the idea of immortality has become an indelible part of church teaching ever since.

What happens when people die? Theologians have speculated about various possible answers to this question, even though they have no personal experience to draw from. Some people claim to have returned to life after they died, and have stories to tell about it. There is no good reason to believe them. Some traditions say that upon death there are only two places

---

27. Quoted by Kaufman, "Existentialism and Death," 48.

to go, heaven or hell, and often claim to be certain who goes where. Some theologians with a universalist bent agree that two such places exist, but on account of Christ's triumphant death and resurrection, hell is empty. Some traditions—Roman Catholic and others—teach that there are three or more destinations for the dead—heaven, hell, and purgatory. Purgatory is an intermediate state where the departed saints, forgiven their mortal sins, are being prepared for heaven by a punishing process of purgation or purification of venial sins. Luther condemned the idea of purgatory not only because it lacked support in the canonical Scriptures, but also because of the rampant abuse of clerical power. Further questions needed to be answered, it seemed. What about unbaptized infants? There is a place for them—limbo of infants, somewhere between heaven and hell. And then there is another limbo for the souls of the patriarchs and saints of the Old Testament. Such speculation may seem harmless; it may also be harmful. There are things about which it is wise to remain agnostic, things that lie beyond the scope of what God has revealed in the Scriptures.

The Devil, Enemy of God

We have discussed sin and death. The third great enemy of humankind is the diabolical enemy of God from before the creation of the world—the devil, known by other appellations in the Scriptures, such as Satan, Lucifer, Adversary, Prince of this world, Prince of darkness, Beelzebub, roaring Lion, Accuser, Dragon, Serpent, the god of this world. Judging from the works attributed to him in the Bible, he's got a very bad reputation. The question is unavoidable, if God created the world good, why is there so much wickedness and wretchedness in the world and all around us?

The devil has become a very controversial fellow. He is also very clever. As C. S. Lewis famously said, "It is the policy of the Devil to persuade us there is no Devil."[28] If the modern consensus is that the devil does not exist, he is given free rein to do his dastardly works behind our backs. We ignore the apostolic warning at our peril: "Be sober, be watchful. Your adversary the devil prowls around like a roaring lion, seeking someone to devour."[29] To delete the devil from Christian discourse does nothing to mitigate the monstrous evils that plagued the world in our lifetime—the devilish

28. Quoted by Russell, *Mephistopheles*, 80.
29. 1 Peter 5:8.

deeds done by Hitler, Stalin, Mao Tse Tung, and Pol Pot—genocide, mass starvation, nuclear missiles, and napalm. The daily news reports *ad nauseam* the crushing evils and perils of racism, xenophobia, oppression, violence, global warming, homelessness, etc. There is no question that these conditions exist.

The Scriptures provide a rich apocalyptic menu of images to speak about the powers behind the scenes—Satan, demons, angels, principalities, dominions, thrones, elemental spirits, the Dragon and the Beast. The biblical story line is the cosmic struggle between the Lord of life and light and the Prince of death and darkness. To neglect the multi-dimensional symbols of the apocalyptic imagination we have in the biblical story of damnation and redemption results in a flattened out, one-dimensional monochromatic universe as uninspiring as it is boring. Post-Enlightenment Protestant theology since Friedrich Schleiermacher eliminated the devil from the Christian belief system. When Paul Tillich published his article entitled, "The Concept of the Demonic and Its Significance for Systematic Theology,"[30] Rudolf Bultmann, the New Testament demythologizer, expressed alarm that Tillich would still use a term from an obsolete worldview. Tillich defined the demonic as a "structure of destruction." He did not think of demons as weightless imps flitting about in the air, occasionally invading human space from the outside. Tillich used the word *structure* in the sense of a "*Gestalt*," a unified whole whose qualities are more than the sum of its component parts. An example would be the anti-Semitic phobia dominating Hitler's Germany that led to the killing of six million Jews.

Tillich was not alone in retrieving the forbidden language about the demonic forces of evil. C. S. Lewis in *The Screwtape Letters* and also in *Perelandra* wrote about the cosmic antagonism between good and evil, convinced that the material physical world is not all there is. There is a world of truths and values beyond what we can see with our ordinary eyes or dissect by reason alone. The same materialistic worldview that breeds the atheistic delusion that God does not exist pays the devil the same compliment.

Georges Bernanos was a member of the Catholic Renaissance in France in the twentieth century along with other notables as François Mauriac, Paul Claudel, and Antoine Peguy. For Bernanos the conflict between good and

---

30. Tillich, "Der Begriff des Dämonischen."

5. SIN, DEATH, AND THE DEVIL

evil in personal experience is the microcosm of the macrocosmic battle between God and the devil. He writes about a deep abyss in human experience "exuding hatred of God and love of death. Deadly sin lies in associating ourselves with nothingness, with a conscious complicity in Satan's ruses, a lucid acceptance of his power to corrupt and a willingness to come to terms with him."[31] Bernanos wrote novels that depict Satan at the heart of evil and Christ at the heart of good. He argued, "Without belief in Satan, one cannot fully believe in God. The world is riddled with evil, and deliberate blindness to that fact obscures the truth about the world and therefore the truth about God. The scale of evil in the world far transcends what humanity could cause itself, and all efforts to improve the world without understanding this transcendence are doomed to failure."[32]

The devil or Satan has been an indelible part of traditional theology since the Bible was written, in Eastern Orthodoxy, Roman Catholicism, and Reformation Protestantism. We have to ask by what authority does a church or its theologians delete this or that from the sum of Christian doctrine so strongly supported by the scriptural narrative in both Testaments? Renewal and reform, yes, but removal and rejection, no! Note what Martin Luther wrote, "It has taken me a long time to discover that it is an article of faith that the Devil is the ruler of this world, the god of this age."[33] The writings of the Fathers, Saints, Mystics, Scholastics, and Reformers are full of images and symbols that portray the devil. It is not possible to subtract the devil, along with demons and angels, without distorting the shape of the Christian faith, and the writing of dogmatics should play no part in that. The Apostle Paul wrote, "The god of this world has blinded the minds of unbelievers, to keep them from seeing the light of the gospel of the glory of Christ, who is the likeness of God."[34] Taking the devil away diminishes the victory of Christ. Guided by the christological rule, we are to judge everything in the light of Christ, in accordance with Luther's dictum, "*Was Christum treibt*!" Take the law away, and there is no need for the gospel! Take sin away, and there is no need for forgiveness. Take death away, and there is no need for resurrection! The chief concern of the New Testament is to tell the good news of the gospel that Christ has gained the victory in

31. Russell, *Mephistopheles*, 276.
32. Russell, *Mephistopheles*, 277.
33. Luther, "Against the Antinomians," 113–14.
34. 2 Corinthians 4:4.

his encounter with sin, death, and the devil. Even in his death on the cross Jesus "disarmed the principalities and powers and made a public example of them, triumphing over them."[35]

The early Christians understood from the Apostle Paul that "they were not contending against flesh and blood, but against the principalities, against the powers, against the world rulers of this present darkness, against the spiritual hosts of wickedness in the heavenly places" and were encouraged to "quench all the flaming darts of the evil one."[36] The Epistles contain innumerable admonitions to withstand "the wiles of the Devil."[37] The first Christians had to endure persecutions from the outside and heresies from the inside. They believed these were the works of the devil and his servant, the Antichrist. But they lived by hope and the promise that in the end the devil will be cast into a "lake of fire" and his power will be no more.[38]

Many present-day Christians seem to be embarrassed by the thought that they are called to be engaged in the cosmic battle between God and the devil. They have gotten used to living in a quiet peaceful town, getting up in the morning to a new day of work and play, turning on the TV, reading the paper, enjoying a cup of coffee, walking the dog, and sending the kids off to school. Talk about the devil and demons, powers and principalities—all of that seems far-fetched and pointless. Then reality strikes. We come to our senses and realize that when our masks are stripped away, our contemporaries, even members of our own family, are victims of addictions, depression, anorexia, bulimia, drugs, alcoholism, lusts, gambling, and they make the rounds of doctors, counselors, therapists, trying every cockamamie prescription to acquire health and happiness. All of these things are plausibly more than a matter of bad luck, bad genes, or bad choices. Christians are free to believe in the active presence of a real personal force, with intelligence and will, at work to corrupt the entire created world and everyone in it. At the same time they know by faith that though the devil is strong, Jesus is stronger, and he proved it in his life and ministry, death and resurrection.

35. 1 Corinthians 2:8.
36. Ephesians 6:12 and 16b.
37. Ephesians 6:11.
38. Revelation 20:20.

5. SIN, DEATH, AND THE DEVIL

Questions for Discussion

1. In the Bible "sin" is understood as a religious concept, not primarily as a moral concept. Is this a true statement? Why, or why not?

2. Karl Menninger, a Christian psychologist, wrote a book entitled, *Whatever Became of Sin?* What is your answer to the question, "Whatever became of sin in American Christianity, in preaching today, and in personal piety?"

3. The New Testament uses a number of Greek words for "sin." Explain the meaning of sin, say, to a confirmation class or in a sermon to a bunch of teenagers at Bible camp.

4. Pelagius and Augustine had different views of "original and hereditary sin." If you were to restart the debate, whose side would you take and why?

5. Martin Luther once said that the best book he ever wrote was *The Bondage of the Will*. Many Lutherans since have not been wholly supportive of his views. What is the issue at stake?

6. If you were asked to preach at the funeral of a Christian friend, how would you deal with the concepts of "immortality of the soul" and "resurrection of the body"?

7. Why do you think many people who have no problem believing in the existence of God find it difficult to believe in the existence of the devil?

6. The Person of Christ

Jesus of Nazareth was born in Bethlehem approximately 4 BC and died in Jerusalem 29 AD. The New Testament is the primary source document that tells the story about the life and ministry of Jesus as well as his crucifixion and resurrection, from the perspective of those who first believed in him as the Christ. Jesus called twelve disciples to join him in his itinerant ministry and was known by his contemporaries as a teacher (rabbi), preacher, baptizer, healer, and miracle worker. His true identity became a matter of controversy. On one occasion he asked his disciples, "Who do people say that I am?"[1] They replied they were not sure. Some confused him with John the Baptist, others with Elijah *redivivus*, still others as one of the prophets. Then Jesus turned to Peter and asked him, "But who do you say that I am?" Peter answered him, "You are the Christ." For the last two thousand years billions of people who shared that belief have been baptized in the name of Jesus the Christ and promised to follow him.

What Is Christology?

Christology is the discipline that aims to produce a comprehensive interpretation of the identity and meaning of Jesus Christ, based on the Holy Scriptures, the ancient creeds of the church, and the history of Christian theology in light of contemporary knowledge and the experience of preaching the gospel to the nations. Both reason and faith cooperate in formulating christological ideas and propositions that inform and edify the present-day community of believers. That Jesus was a historical figure, a Jewish rabbi, who lived and died in Palestine two thousand-some years ago is a subject of biographical interest to research historians. That he is the Son of God, the Lord Jesus Christ, who was raised from the dead and reigns at the right hand of his Father is exclusively a matter of faith. A majority of people know that

1. Mark 8:27–29.

6. THE PERSON OF CHRIST

he lived and died once upon a time. Only a minority believe that he is alive and at work in the world today. Biographers, Christian or not, have written biographies of Jesus. Muslims, Hindus, Sikhs, and Buddhists have their own views and opinions concerning Jesus of Nazareth. Christology is not a biography, though it certainly does include reference to historical events in the life of Jesus. Christology is essentially an intellectually constructed confessional statement of faith based on divinely revealed truth, enabled by the inner testimony of the Holy Spirit. Faith in Jesus as the Christ of God is not dependent on the results of scientific inquiry into the historical Jesus. Thinking that it so is due to a colossal misunderstanding of Christology's role. Sound historical research can report that the earliest sources and traditions concerning Jesus of Nazareth portray him as more than a man, as the anointed Christ of God, even as the Word of God in the flesh, who was with God in the beginning and who was God.[2] It is impossible to elevate Jesus of Nazareth—one who is truly human—to a higher level, one who is different from all other human beings not only by degree but also by nature, by partaking of the divine nature. And what did doubting Thomas say when the risen Jesus appeared to him? He exclaimed, "My Lord and my God!"

The *content* of Christology only makes sense within the *context* of the Christian community, to inform and norm its worship and witness. The christological dogma of Jesus Christ as both God and man guides the church and its preaching today to represent the saving message of the gospel in a faithful and powerful way. The Creed of Chalcedon reads: "We all with one voice teach that it should be confessed that our Lord Jesus Christ is one and the same Son, the Same perfect in Godhead, the Same perfect in manhood, truly God and truly man."[3] Traditionally dogmaticians—both Roman Catholic and Reformation Protestant—started their christological reflections by citing this dogma of the one person of Jesus Christ in two natures. After treating the dogma of the Trinity it was customary to proceed to the dogma of the incarnation of the Son of God. That is doing Christology deductively "from above."

Modern Christology has responded to the pressure of critics of the dogma who argued that it lacked support in the real Jesus of history. After all, the dogma claimed to assert the truth about Jesus in his earthly life and

2. John 1:1–14.
3. Sellers, *The Council of Chalcedon*, 210.

ministry. Its intent was not to make things up; it was not self-authenticating; it was not true simply because a majority of conciliar bishops voted in its favor. Furthermore, even if the christological dogma could claim support in the kerygmatic preaching of the apostles recorded in the New Testament, that still leaves open the question whether it is grounded in the words and acts of the historical Jesus. The theological task is to show the linkage between three essential components of a full Christology—the Jesus of history, the apostolic kerygma, and church dogma. The strategy to accomplish this task is to do Christology inductively "from below." This means to trace the christological trajectory backwards, from dogma and kerygma back to the Jesus of history. So the place to begin christological thinking today is exactly where it all began in the first place—with Jesus himself.

The Life and Ministry of Jesus

How did it come about that this Jewish rabbi and prophet who met his fate as a common criminal on a Roman cross would soon thereafter be lauded as King, Messiah, Lord, Savior, Son of God, and the very Word (Logos) who was with God and who, indeed, was God? What was there about Jesus' life and his self-understanding that evoked such honorific epithets from his disciples and apostles? Jesus did not walk the dusty roads of Palestine claiming such glorious titles for himself. There is no explicit Christology in his teaching and preaching. He did not say, "I am Jesus Christ, the great Jesus Christ Superstar!" Yet, there may have been an implicit Christology in the original Jesus that provided a point of contact for the subsequent explicit Christology in the New Testament Gospels and Epistles. Preaching Jesus as the Christ and praising him as really God are either true interpretations or they are misrepresentations, as some critics with a "low Christology" allege. It would be implausible to maintain that the earliest believers arbitrarily attributed christological titles to Jesus without any motivating factor in his own public ministry.

Jesus began his ministry in Galilee preaching "the gospel of God, and saying, 'The time is fulfilled, and the kingdom of God is at hand; repent, and believe in the gospel.'"[4] Jesus' earliest followers who became believers in him as the Christ remembered that he addressed God as "Abba," expressing the most intimate personal relation to his Father. The way in which he did

4. Mark 1:14–15.

this was something new, in comparison with what we find in his Hebrew Bible and the Judaism of his day. His relation to his Father implies his Sonship in an exclusive sense. He is uniquely the one and only begotten Son of God, and not merely one among the many children of the heavenly Father who pray the Lord's Prayer, "Our Father who art in heaven." The Father-Son relationship is the foundation of the reconciliation of all people with God and with one another. Thus, the root of Christology is Jesus' relationship to Abba, his Father, like unto none other.

There is virtual consensus among New Testament scholars that the idea of the kingdom (rule or reign) of God is at the heart of Jesus' message. His words (parables) and acts (miracles) were "signs" of the inbreaking power of God's reign. Jesus announced the imminent approach of God's kingdom; it was near at hand. Its advance signs were already visible in his ministry. What is more, Jesus bound the coming of the kingdom to his person. In a real sense, Jesus belongs to the gospel he preached. Origen of Alexandria (third century) used the term *autobasileia* to express the idea that Jesus is himself the kingdom. He is in person the decisive event inaugurating the rule of God in world history. The unconditional promise of salvation is expressed in Jesus' authority to forgive sins, to declare sinners acceptable in God's eyes, to bless the poor and heal the sick. A prophet cries out, "Thus saith the Lord!" But Jesus said, "Truly I say unto you!" A rabbi interprets the Scriptures, appealing to their authority. Jesus took authority unto himself and said, "You have heard it said of old, but I say unto you." He spoke with immediate and direct authority, announcing the coming of God's reign in and through his words and actions. The relation of the kingdom he preached is so close to his earthly ministry that his death on the cross was seen *ex post facto* as his enthronement as King.

Death and Resurrection

There are two additional events in the story of Jesus that gave rise to subsequent apostolic reverencing of Jesus as Christ and Lord—his death on the cross and his resurrection from the dead. This double ending of his life is the *sine qua non* of all the honorific titles ascribed to him in the New Testament. This was the good news of the gospel of salvation that the first apostolic missionaries left Jerusalem to tell to the nations. On account of his resurrection, Jesus was present in the power of the Holy Spirit as the living Lord and loving Savior. Starting from below with the human Jesus, the conviction that God raised him from the dead eventually propelled the confession that he is the Christ and finally to the highest possible identification of Jesus as truly God. Jesus' personal identity as truly God is the root of the creedal doctrine of the Holy Trinity.

Jesus began his public ministry proclaiming that the kingdom of God was coming soon, so soon that its initial inbreaking was already taking place. Thus Jesus said, "But if it is by the finger of God that I cast out demons, then the kingdom of God has come upon you."[5] Jesus did not preach that the kingdom of God was already fulfilled in his ministry. When the kingdom comes in its fullness, everything must change and will change. The radical change begins with repentance, turning away from the old and welcoming the new. "Repent, for the kingdom of heaven is at hand."[6] The Great Commandment is at the heart of the revolutionary morality Jesus had in mind. Love God in an absolute way, and love your neighbor as yourself. The moral imperative is one-sided, for the love of God goes first to those in terrible need of repentance—sinners, publicans (quislings), prostitutes, and non-kosher people. Jesus brings forgiveness to them. He was called out for doing that. "Who is this, who even forgives sins?"[7] Every good Scribe and Pharisee believed that only God can forgive sins. "Why does this man speak thus? It is blasphemy! Who can forgive sins but God alone?"[8] Jesus was accused by the religious leaders of his day of pretending to be God. If that is not indeed true, he would be not only an impostor but a blasphemer. C. S. Lewis said something to the effect that if Jesus was not the one he claimed to be, he was either a liar or a lunatic. So, speaking to liberal humanists, Lewis told them to stop the nonsense of saying Jesus was a great teacher of morality, but certainly not the Messiah or Son of God.

Jesus ended his ministry of teaching and healing with his death on the cross. He died at the hands of many forces. The heads of organized religion, high priests and elders, conspired with the established secular rulers, King Herod and Governor Pilate, to put Jesus on trial and condemn him to death. The mob fell in line with the ruling class, chanting "crucify him." Soldiers

5. Luke 11:20.
6. Matthew 3:2.
7. Luke 7:49b.
8. Mark 2:7.

carried out the verdict of the corrupt judicial system. They stripped him naked, beat him almost to death, and pressed a crown of thorns into his scalp. An innocent man was made the victim of capital punishment. Jesus' death was horrible, ugly, and unjust. It might have been written up in the obituary section of the morning gazette as the fate of another criminal. But the cross of Jesus acquired a different meaning after his resurrection. A great reversal took place in the mind of God his Father. Jesus' death on the cross was credited as life and salvation for the world, for all. "He died for all, that those who live might no longer live for themselves but for him who for their sake died and was raised."[9] "Jesus gave himself for our sins to set us free from the present evil age, according to the will of God our Father."[10] "Jesus himself bore our sins in his body on the cross."[11]

For the Gospel writers the death and resurrection of Jesus was the fulfillment of the kingdom he had expected in the nearest possible future—paradoxically hidden under the sign of the cross. For them this was proof, blessed with new eyes of faith, that Jesus was the long expected Messiah and the King of the kingdom he preached. The Jesus of history is the Christ of faith indivisibly and inseparably, as the Creed of Chalcedon confesses. Reason can learn certain things about the historical Jesus with some degree of probability, but only faith can know with assurance that shalom and salvation have reached the world in his name. The angel said to Joseph, "You shall call his name Jesus, for he will save his people from their sins."[12]

The early Christians believed that the kingdom had already arrived in Jesus' life, ministry, death, and resurrection, yet it seemed obvious to them that the world remained the same. Life went on pretty much as usual; nothing had visibly changed for the better. Poverty, sickness, depression, decay, degradation, death, greed, corruption, violence, wars, racism, sexism, and xenophobia abounded all around. In what sense then has the kingdom come? The kingdom has already come in the name of Jesus wherever forgiven sinners receive the gifts of the Holy Spirit—"Love, joy, peace, patience, kindness, goodness, faithfulness, gentleness, self-control . . . and those who belong to

---

9. 2 Corinthians 5:15.
10. Galatians 1:4.
11. 1 Peter 2:24.
12. Matthew 1:21.

Christ Jesus have crucified the flesh with its passions and desires."[13] We can know the kingdom has already come in Jesus' name when the hungry are fed, the thirsty are given drink, strangers are welcomed, the naked are clothed, and the sick and imprisoned are visited. These things are already happening as signs of the presence of the kingdom, but the ultimate fulfillment of the kingdom is yet to come. The first Christians became aware that they were living between the times, between the "already" and the "not yet," already living in the afterglow of Easter, yet longing for the *parousia* still to come, the final advent of Jesus to judge the living and the dead.

The Divine Identity of Jesus of Nazareth

The fourth-century confession of the Nicene Creed that Jesus Christ is "true God from true God" and "of one Being with the Father" would not (could not) have been made apart from the apostolic belief that Jesus rose from the dead on the third day. Only the God who created the world has the power to save it from its bondage to sin, death, and the devil. The logic is airtight: if Jesus is the Savior of the world, he must be God. In his public ministry Jesus challenged the rule of Satan by casting out demons. On the cross of Jesus God was dealing with the sin of the world. In Jesus' resurrection death was conquered by new life. After Easter the communities founded by the apostles addressed Jesus in their prayers and petitions in ways that belonged only to God, which would be idolatrous if it were not appropriate. In the second century St. Clement of Rome wrote, "We must think of Jesus Christ as of God."[14] The Apostle Paul said that the name of Jesus is exalted above every name.[15] When the early Christians addressed Jesus as Lord (*kyrios*), they were not merely using a polite form of address. *Kyrios* was the Greek translation of the Hebrew *Adonai*, the most common Jewish name for God.

To confess that Jesus is Lord in a Jewish worship setting could only mean one thing—Jesus is one with God embodied in human form. Once this transaction happened the earliest Christian communities were well on their way to transfer all the attributes of God to Jesus, not only those related to redemption but also to creation. Note what St. Paul says in his letter

13. Galatians 5:22–24
14. 2 Clement 1:1.
15. Philippians 2:9.

6. THE PERSON OF CHRIST

to the Colossians: "He is the image of the invisible God, the first-born of all creation; for in him all things were created, in heaven and on earth, visible and invisible, whether thrones or dominions or principalities or authorities—all things were created through him and for him. He is before all things, and in him all things hold together."[16]

It is not surprising that such an extraordinary shift in language usage—speaking of the other-worldliness of God in this-worldly human terms—would generate some confusion and controversy. If Jesus was really divine, maybe he was not really human. Docetism is the name of the early heresy (first century) that asserts it is not possible to be both divine and human at the same time. *Docetism* is a word that stems from the Greek word *dokein*, meaning "to seem." Docetic Christology asserts that Jesus is truly God but only seems to be human. He only appeared to suffer and die as a human being of flesh and blood. The Docetists had no problem affirming the divinity of Christ. It was his humanity they called into question. But the pendulum could swing to the opposite side, and it did so in the teaching of Ebionitism. Ebionitism, old and new, treats Jesus as a real human being. It's his divinity the Ebionites could not allow. The Docetists came from a Greek orientation, whereas the Ebionites came from a Jewish background. These are the two heretical extremes that seem to be polar opposite. However, the result is the same—they both reject a real incarnation of God in the man Jesus. Because God is infinite, immortal, and eternal, it is presumed to be ontologically impossible for God to enter the experience of a finite, mortal, and temporal being. Docetists and Ebionites agree on the axiom—the finite is not capable of the infinite *(finitum non capax Infiniti)*.

The docetic and ebionitic trends never died down and continue to have their followers in present-day theology.[17] The docetic trend reappeared in the teaching of Sabellius (third century), known as Modalistic Monarchianism, also as Patripassianism. Modalism rejects the tripersonal Trinity and instead teaches that the one God (Monarch) appeared in three modes of appearance (wearing three masks), as the Father in creation, the Son in redemption, and the Spirit in sanctification. The Ebionitic trend reappeared in the teaching of Paul of Samosata, bishop of Antioch (third century), known as Adoptionism. Adoptionism, like Modalistic

---

16. Colossians 1:15–17.
17. See Hick, ed., *The Myth of God Incarnate*.

Monarchianism, is another form of unitarianism, that denies that Jesus is the eternal Son of God. Rather, Jesus supposedly became the Son of God by adoption, by virtue of his perfect obedience to his Father's will and steady growth in spiritual and moral qualities of life.

Christological Heresies

At this point in our discussion it is important to insert a caveat. In the history of Christianity the names of individual theologians are customarily attached to certain heresies, which they were accused of teaching. Thus, Sabellianism was named after Sabellius, who was accused of teaching the heresy of Modalistic Monarchianism and Patripassianism. Church historians have debated the question whether Sabellius was really guilty of teaching Sabellianism, or whether he was instead the victim of misrepresentation by his church political opponents. Friedrich Schleiermacher issued the warning that in dogmatics we are not dealing with the historical question whether the heretical "isms" were actually taught by the theologians accused of teaching them. "But these names are here intended only to denote universal forms which we are here going to unfold, and the definitions of which they are intended to remind us proceed from the general nature of the situation, even if, e. g., Pelagius himself should not be a Pelagian in our sense."[18]

The ancient church struggled long and hard to develop a Christology that would be strong enough to support the apostolic gospel of salvation. There were two schools of thought driving the debates of the fourth and fifth centuries that culminated in a number of church councils, each promulgating a creed with accompanying anathemas. One school was located in Antioch of Syria and the other in Alexandria of Egypt. The Antiochian theologians tended to stress the full humanity of Jesus Christ whereas the Alexandrian theologians were equally zealous to stress the full divinity of Jesus Christ. They were confronted with the problem, which loomed as a mystery, as to how the divine nature of Jesus as the Son of God and the human nature of Jesus of Nazareth born of the Virgin Mary could be united in one person. The logic of salvation required that the one person of Jesus Christ must be fully God who alone has the power to save and he must also be fully human—in body, mind, and spirit—all that which is in need of a full salvation.

18. Schleiermacher, *The Christian Faith*, 97.

6. THE PERSON OF CHRIST

At the Council of Nicaea in 325 AD, Arianism was condemned as a heresy. Arius was a priest who taught that the Logos, the second person of the Trinity, was not the eternal Son of God, essentially equal with God the Father. He was the first creature, created by God to assist in the creation of the world. Before he was there was God alone, thereby affirming the principle of Monarchianism, i.e. Unitarianism. Arius was vehemently attacked by Athanasius, bishop of Alexandria, who insisted on a real incarnation of God. Not any being less than God would be qualified to be the Redeemer. Athanasius argued that the Mediator between God and humanity needs to be fully divine and fully human, to accomplish a real salvation. The Council of Nicaea, AD 325, decreed that Jesus Christ is "eternally begotten of the Father . . . true God from true God"—a clear negation of Arianism.

After the Council of Nicaea the search for an adequate Christology continued, still pondering how one who is fully divine can be incarnate in the human being of Jesus. Apollinaris, a friend of Athanasius, and fully in accord with the trinitarian Creed of Nicaea, was a fierce opponent of Arius. The Son who is eternally one with the Father became incarnate. But how? Apollinaris shared the Platonic trichotomous view that a human being consists of body, mind, and spirit. Apollinaris was concerned to affirm that the divine and human natures become united *in one person*. His solution—when the Logos became incarnate, he displaced the human spirit, clothing himself only with the human body and mind. Hence, he was accused of docetism, because without a human spirit, Jesus would be lacking an essential part of being human, something equally in need of salvation. The Council of Constantinople (AD 38) condemned Apollinarianism because it denied the full humanity of Jesus. The logic of salvation again prevailed in the thinking of the Council fathers. What was not assumed cannot be saved. The Council declared that it is necessary for the Savior to be fully human, because the whole person needs salvation, spirit as well as mind and body.

In a short time the pendulum swung to the opposite side. The Antiochian school traditionally emphasized an untruncated view of the humanity of Jesus. Nestorius, patriarch of Constantinople, affirmed the conciliar confessions of Nicaea and Constantinople—Jesus Christ is consubstantial with the Father and equally consubstantial with humanity, truly God and truly Man. For Nestorius this meant that the Savior must be endowed with two of everything—two natures, two wills, both divine and human attributes, and therefore also two persons. How could Jesus be fully human if he were not a human person? Impossible, he thought, for the Gospels clearly tell the story of the words and deeds of a human person, in association with all sorts of other human persons, some friends, some foes. In the incarnation two persons—divine and human—are acting in the closest possible communion in the life and ministry of Jesus.

The dualistic two-person scheme of Nestorianism was quickly attacked by theologians of Alexandria, accusing it of teaching that Jesus was a mere man, the perennial charge against the Antiochian school. In the incarnation there must be a *union* of God and Man, not merely a *communion* between two persons. Eutyches was the patriarch of Constantinople who led the charge against Nestorianism. He taught that in the incarnation the divine nature assumed the human nature into itself, resulting in only one nature. His teaching is called monophysitism—one nature! Jesus, the Lord and Savior of the world, is God pure and simple.

Entering the fifth century, church theologians were deeply divided. The school of Alexandria favored the divinity of Christ at the expense of his humanity. The school of Antioch favored the humanity of Jesus at the expense of his divinity. The Alexandrian school had to cope with such heretical isms as Docetism, Modalistic Monarchianism, Sabellianism, Patripassianism, Apollinarianism, Monophysitism, and Eutycheanism. The Antiochian school was associated with the isms of Ebionitism, Adoptionism, Arianism, and Nestorianism. There is dogmatic significance in knowing these isms and how they misconstrue the Christian faith because they are not mere relics of ancient history but get repeated in subsequent history as well as today in various configurations. Some liberal Protestant theologians disbelieve the doctrine of the Trinity and the divinity of Christ. Gnostic Christianity, based on the extant Gnostic Gospels, portrays Jesus of Nazareth as a figure neither fully divine nor fully human.

The Two Natures of Christ

Ecumenical Christian dogmatics works constructively within the boundaries of the following Creed of Chalcedon, AD 451.

> Following, then, the holy Fathers, we unite in teaching all men to confess the one and only Son, our Lord Jesus Christ. This selfsame

> one is perfect both in deity and also in human-ness; this selfsame one is also actually God and actually man, with a rational soul and a body. He is of the same reality as God as far as his deity is concerned and of the same reality as we are ourselves as far as his human-ness is concerned; thus like us in all respect, sin only excepted. Before time began he was begotten of the Father, in respect to his deity, and now in these last days, for us and for our salvation, this selfsame one was born of Mary the virgin, who is God-bearer (*theotokos*) in respect to his human-ness.
>
> We also teach that we apprehend this one and only Christ—Son, Lord, only-begotten—in two natures; and we do this without confusing the two natures, without transmuting one nature into the other, without dividing them into two separate categories, without contrasting them according to area or function. The distinctiveness of each nature is not nullified by the union. Instead, the properties of each nature are conserved and both natures concur in one person (*prosopon*) and in one *hypostasis* (substance). They are not divided or cut into two persons (*prosopa*), but are together the one and only-begotten Logos of God, the Lord Jesus Christ. Thus have the prophets of old testified; thus the Lord Jesus Christ himself taught us; thus the Symbol of the Fathers has handed down to us.

This Creed does not explain the mystery of the incarnation. It cannot be comprehended by any philosophical system, theory of psychology, or biological science. The Creed is affirming a true incarnation of the Son of God in a real human being whose life story is narrated in the four Gospels of the New Testament. All of the heresies cited above were anathematized because they failed to accomplish that, veering either to the right, emphasizing Jesus' God-ness, or to the left, emphasizing Jesus' human-ness. After Chalcedon theologians continued to speculate how the infinite nature of the eternal God could become united with the finite nature of a temporal human being in the one person of Jesus Christ. It's like trying to put a square peg in a round hole, squaring the circle, attempting the impossible. Theologians felt free to try and they did.

The Creed of Chalcedon established that no Christology would be acceptable to the church for the sake of its mission to preach the gospel of salvation that failed to affirm that the person of Jesus Christ is fully God, of one Being with the Father, and fully human, like unto us in every respect, except without sin. Still, this consensus did not prevent a flare-up of controversy among Reformation Protestants in the sixteenth century, between Lutherans and Calvinists. The occasion was the historic disagreement over the Lord's Supper. Luther taught that in Holy Communion the whole Christ in both natures was really present, including his body and blood. Luther cited the very words of Jesus at the Last Supper, "Take, eat; this is my body."[19] Huldreich Zwingli, a Swiss Reformer, replied with his theory of *alloeosis*, which is to say that Jesus was only using a figure of speech, and did not intend his words to be taken literally. The human Christ, Zwingli averred, cannot be present in the Lord's Supper, because to be human is to be finite, and a finite body cannot be in many places at one and the same time. That is palpably true, except that Luther came back with his theory of ubiquity. Ubiquity or omnipresence is properly an attribute of Christ's divine nature, but in the incarnation this attribute is communicated to the human nature. The Lutheran doctrine of the communication of attributes (*communicatio idiomatum*) was developed to reinforce the traditional catholic liturgical belief that what is given in the Holy Supper is not merely bread and wine but also the body and blood of the whole Christ.

In the period of the Enlightenment the floodgates of criticism were opened to wash away virtually every doctrine in the Christian tradition. The criticisms were many and varied. Critical historians tried to replace the christological dogma with a biography of Jesus. "Lives of Jesus" became best-sellers, some of them written in a spirit of hostility to Christianity, some highly skeptical of the historical reliability of the Gospels, and some sympathetic with Jesus as a great moral example and teacher.[20] Philosophers attacked traditional Christology for its use of obsolete Greek concepts and terms such as *homoousios, hypostasis, ousia, physis*, and *prosopon*, which are moreover unintelligible in this modern age. Even serious theologians with good will worried that Christology had become conceptually so complex that it threatened to eclipse the simple teachings of Jesus and the message of the gospel.

One impressive compromise was attempted by the German Lutheran theologian Gottfried Thomasius (1802–1875), to incorporate the modern picture of the historical Jesus into the framework of the Lutheran doctrine of the "communication of attributes." He attempted this by using the idea of

---

19. Matthew 26:26.
20. See Schweitzer, *The Quest of the Historical Jesus*.

"kenosis" in Philippians 2: 6–7: "Who though he was in the form of God, did not count equality with God a thing to be grasped, but emptied (*ékenösen*) himself, taking the form of a servant, being born in the likeness of men." He emptied himself, that is, in Thomasius's interpretation, the Logos divested himself of all the divine omni-attributes (omnipotence, omnipresence, etc.) and humbled himself in becoming a man, endowed exclusively with human attributes. This kenotic Christology was radicalized to the point that the Son of God was thought to have surrendered all traces of his divinity in the incarnation. If that is what happened—a question was posed as a criticism—in what sense was Jesus of Nazareth anything more than a man, not really God at all? The solution did not work, for it suggested that for God to become man he had to cease being God.

In spite of all such criticisms the traditional christological dogma retains its validity in present-day theology and Christianity. First of all, it is a strong statement of what Christians in good faith do not believe concerning Jesus Christ. The left-wing teaching concerning Jesus as a "mere man," represented by Ebionitism, Adoptionism, and Nestorianism,[21] is not and will never be true to the portrayals of Jesus in the New Testament and the first Christians, some of them eyewitnesses, apostles, and evangelists. Similarly, the right-wing teaching in line with Docetism, Modalism, Sabellianism, Apollinarianism, and Eutycheanism fails to do justice to a real incarnation of the Logos in the flesh of a real human being. The Creed does positively encapsulate the gospel truth that God took on a truly human reality in Jesus Christ, the Mediator between the Almighty Creator and the fallen creation. Those who confess this truth will joyfully believe, teach, and confess that in Jesus Christ God participates in the human condition for the salvation of humanity and the eschatological fulfillment of history and the world.

Questions for Discussion

1. What is the basic difference between a theologian writing a Christology and a biographer writing a "Life of Jesus"?
2. Identify and describe the essential components of a full Christology.

---

21. Again, it is important to note that the use of the term *Nestorianism* does not settle the historical question whether Nestorius was himself a "Nestorian," as he was accused by his church political opponents. Cf. Braaten, "Modern Interpretations of Nestorius."

3. What are the most historically reliable sources for our knowledge of Jesus of Nazareth?

4. The Apostles' Creed confesses that "Jesus rose from the dead." How can we know if this is historically true or merely an ancient myth?

5. What is Docetism? What is Ebionitism?

6. Name three christological heresies and explain why the ancient councils of the church rejected them as false teaching.

7. Why did the Christians of the first five centuries come to believe that Jesus of Nazareth is more than a human being, truly the incarnation of God and of one being with God the Father?

7. The Work of Christ

The doctrine of the work of Christ has traditionally focused on his crucifixion and interpreted in various theories of the atonement. The main orthodox doctrine of the atonement in both the Catechism of the Roman Catholic Church and the Catechisms of the Reformed and Lutheran traditions focus on the sacrificial death of Jesus on the cross, rendering satisfaction to the triune God, whose absolute justice required penalties proportionate to the sins of humankind offensive to God's will. To concentrate exclusively on the crucifixion does not do justice to the whole reconciling work of Christ from his pre-existence before the creation of the world to his final return from heaven to judge the living and the dead, and all the events in between cited in the Apostles' Creed—his resurrection, descent into hell, ascension, and his session at the right hand of the Father. The point is: Jesus Christ is the person in whom God is acting in history for the salvation of the fallen world. Jesus Christ is the Mediator reconciling the world to God from alpha to omega.

The New Testament and Mythology

The New Testament portrayal of Jesus Christ is set within a Ptolemaic cosmology, picturing a three-storied universe, heaven above, hell below, and the earth in the middle. Jesus came down from heaven, performed his ministry on earth, descended into the netherworld of hell, and ascended to heaven from whence he came. In terms of contemporary literary analysis this ancient three-story picture of the world is mythological. It is confusing to use the word *myth* in connection with the New Testament narrative of the Son of God leaving his pre-existent state in heaven, descending to earth for thirty years, dying on a cross, rising from the dead, then ascending to heaven from whence he came. The word *myth* has become a synonym for a fictitious tale, a made-up story, as in, "That's pure myth; don't believe it." For two thousand years those who have believed in the biblical revelation of God in Jesus Christ do not regard what the four Gospels in the New Testament narrate about Jesus as "pure myth." On the contrary, they believe the story of Jesus Christ is true, the good news of salvation, anything but fiction.

A generation ago Rudolf Bultmann, New Testament theologian from Marburg, Germany, proposed to demythologize the gospel by means of an existentialist interpretation of the mythology.[1] He deemed this to be necessary because modern science has rendered untenable the ancient mythical picture of a three-story universe. Therefore, Bultmann maintained that the demythologizing must be done radically without anything remaining. After much probing analysis and discussion Bultmann's program proved unsatisfactory because he threw the baby out with the bath water, eliminating the gospel with the myth.[2] All that remained was the crucified Jesus, inspiring an existential decision to be crucified with Christ. The Christology that remains is reduced to an "*Imitatio Christi*."

To eliminate the myth *in toto* leaves only the historical event of a crucified man. There is no gospel of salvation in that. The gospel is the message of God who acts in Christ, which from beginning to end is clothed in the language of symbols that may be called mythical in terms of literary genre. The symbols of God and the devil, heaven and hell, descent and ascent, virginal birth, sacrificial death, and bodily resurrection, are all essential elements of a whole narrative that Christology interprets in a soteriological way. The mythology is the envelope, not the letter inside with the message of God who acts in Christ for the salvation of the world. The picture of the world is the literary framework whose purpose is to convey the message of salvation. The point is to interpret every jot and tittle of the whole story, not to eliminate it by calling it mythological. Christian dogmatics is concerned with the soteriological essence of the whole story of the eternal God in Christ, and is not put off by its cosmological wrappings. The great christological tradition at its best has been able to distinguish between the swaddling clothes—what is bound to the time—and the baby in the manger—the essence of the gospel message. *Pace* Marshall McLuhan, the medium is not the message. Only the rankest kind of literalistic fundamentalism might think to the contrary.

1. Bultmann, "New Testament and Mythology."
2. See Braaten and Harrisville, eds., *Kerygma and History*.

7. THE WORK OF CHRIST

The Preexistence of Christ

The key biblical verse that speaks of the pre-existence of Jesus Christ is John 1:14: "And the Word became flesh and dwelt among us, full of grace and truth; we have beheld his glory, glory as of the only Son from the Father." This speaks to the divine identity of Jesus Christ, the very condition of the heavy burden he bore in procuring the salvation of the world through his sufferings and death. But there are other verses that bespeak Jesus' pre-existence. John 8:58 says, "Jesus said to them, 'Truly, truly, I say to you, before Abraham was, I am.'" Jesus also said, "Father, glorify thou me in thy own presence with the glory which I had with thee before the world was made" (John 17:5). The exalted Son of God, Jesus Christ, began his work as the agent of creation and the source of its very life and light. "He was in the beginning with God; all things were made through him, and without him was not anything made that was made. In him was life, and the life was the light of men. The light shines in the darkness, and the darkness has not overcome it." (John 1:2–5.) The pre-existence of Jesus as very God is the preamble of the whole story of salvation in his name. "Who, though he was in the form of God, did not count equality with God a thing to be grasped, but emptied himself, taking on the form of a servant, being born in the likeness of men. And being found in human form he humbled himself and became obedient unto death, even death on a cross." (Philippians 2: 6–8.) All these verses concerning the pre-existence of the Logos incarnate in Jesus emphasize that the salvation he earned for the world originates in the eternal God. The logic of salvation is transparent. Jesus is the Savior of the world. Only God can have the power to save. Jesus is the eternal Son of God sent into the world to save sinners. All the christological heresies discussed above fail to pass the test of soteriology because either they separate the divine and human natures, omitting the union, or they collapse one into the other, denying their difference.

The Virgin Birth

From the beginning of Christianity controversy has swirled around the role of Mary in the story of salvation wrought by Christ. The devotion to Mary, the Mother of the Lord Jesus, snowballed through church history to the point where in some circles of popular piety she receives honor and devotion bordering on worship. Mariology becomes Mariolatry. From the viewpoint of the Reformers, Luther and Calvin, Mary then becomes an idol; she who is not God is worshiped as God. They protested the "abominable idolatry" of medieval Mariology.

In the *Apology of the Augsburg Confession* of 1530 Philip Melanchthon wrote:

> Granted that Mary prays for the church, does she receive souls in death, does she overcome death, does she give life? What does Christ do if blessed Mary does all this? Even though she is worthy of the highest honors, she does not want to be put on the same level as Christ but to have her example considered and followed. The fact of the matter is that in popular estimation the blessed Virgin has completely replaced Christ. Men have invoked her, trusted in her mercy, and sought through her to appease Christ, as though he were not a propitiator, but only a terrible judge and avenger. We maintain that we dare not trust in the transfer of the saints' merits thus, as though God were reconciled to us or accounted us righteous or saved us on this account. We obtain the forgiveness of sins only by Christ's merits when we believe in him.[3]

In this passage Melanchthon was addressing medieval distortions of the official Catholic doctrine of Mary. However, the general reaction to the place of Mary in later Protestant devotion, worship, and theology became excessively negative. Mary was all but completely ignored, for fear that she would be venerated at the expense of Christ. The Reformers, to the contrary, had a high esteem for Mary. Their Confessions called her the Mother of God (*Theotokos*). Luther expounded the *Magnificat* of Luke 1:46–55 and treated Mary as the embodiment of God's unmerited grace. Mary magnified God who is the Father of her Son Jesus. Luther wrote, "Men have crowded all her glory into a single word, calling her the Mother of God (Theotokos). . . . In order to become the Mother of God, she had to be a woman, a virgin, of the tribe of Judah, and had to believe the angelic message in order to become worthy as the Scriptures foretold. . . . Mary does not desire to be an idol; she does nothing, God does all."[4] Luther also retained the traditional Catholic view that Mary remained always a virgin (*semper virgine*), without sin, full of grace, who intercedes for us. Such extolling of Mary was always done on account of the one named Jesus, "for he shall save his people from their

---

3. "Apology of the Augsburg Confession."
4. Luther, "The Magnificat," 326–29.

sins."[5] When we praise and honor Mary we are giving God all the glory for what he chose to do with and through her.

In the periods of Protestant Orthodoxy and Pietism the Marian festivals declined, as well as the invocation of Mary and the saints. Sporadic attempts were made thereafter to revive Luther's high appreciation of Mary. The high church movement in the nineteenth century encouraged a liturgical renewal that included three Marian feasts, Annuniciation, Visitation, and Purification. It restored the practice of Marian devotion, but rejected the new dogmas of the Roman Catholic Church, the Immaculate Conception of Mary (1854) and the Bodily Assumption of Mary (1950). Non-Roman Churches meanwhile continue to resist developments that focus on Mary as Mediatrix and Co-Redemptrist, insofar as these titles seem to grant her an equal share in the redemptive work of Jesus.

The Protestant flight from Mary was checked by the combined impact of the modern ecumenical movement and the liturgical movement. Protestants today who accept the Councils of the ancient church gladly confess, with Luther and the other Reformers, that Mary is the Mother of God.[6] They do this as an implication of the Nicene confession of Jesus as "truly God, of one Being with God," even though the New Testament nowhere calls Mary "Mother of God."

The belief that Jesus was born of a virgin has been rejected by those who think it undercuts his fully humanity, who was like unto us in every respect. The virgin birth has, to the contrary, been affirmed by those who think it supports his full divinity. In the ancient christological debates the virgin birth was affirmed by both sides, the Antiochians and the Alexandrians; by itself it offered no proof positive as to which side was right. The chief point of the miraculous birth is not to draw attention to a biological anomaly—parthenogenesis. That by itself would have no theological significance. The truth of the virginal conception by the Holy Spirit is that God is the source and power of salvation through Christ from the start, at his birth, not only in his atoning death and victorious resurrection.

---

5. Matthew 1:21.
6. See Braaten and Jenson, eds., *Mary, Mother of God*.

Mary was one of the subjects of dialogue between Lutherans and Roman Catholics in the twentieth century,[7] which had become divisive in the period of the Reformation. Their concluding statement showed broad areas of consensus, that many of the traditional divergences may be differences of piety rather than church-dividing doctrines. They agreed that nothing may subtract from the unique mediatorship of Christ, neither Mary nor any of the saints. They reached clarification regarding the invocation of saints; saints are not addressed as saviors or redeemers, which would detract from the power of salvation that belongs to God alone, but as intercessors, in the same way that fellow Christians on earth are addressed when asked to pray for someone or some cause. This depends on the conviction that departed saints are living members of the communion of saints. There is a solidarity of the church militant with the church triumphant that both confessions affirm. Yet, despite their most earnest efforts to reach consensus, the two Marian dogmas—Immaculate Conception and Assumption of Mary—remain as obstacles to fuller convergence. Nevertheless, Lutherans can respect the assurance of their Catholic interlocutors that for them Mariology does not lead to Mariolatry but leads them closer to Christ. Mariology properly understood reinforces Christology. The virgin birth is all about Jesus. The famous Isenheimer Altar painting by Matthias Grünewald shows John the Baptist pointing to Jesus dying on the cross, with the Johannine inscription below, "He must increase, but I must decrease."[8] Mother Mary is also in the picture looking to Jesus, mourning the death of her son.

The Cross of Christ

The Apostle Paul wrote, "For I decided to know nothing among you except Jesus Christ and him crucified."[9] St. Paul was Martin Luther's favorite New Testament author. After he posted his ninety-five theses in Wittenberg (1517), he held a disputation with his fellow Augustinian monks in Heidelberg, in which he echoed the apostle's sentiment: "That person deserves to be called a theologian who comprehends the visible and manifest things of God through suffering and the cross."[10] He also said, "The cross alone is our theology." Luther contrasted a theology of

7. Cf. Anderson, Stafford, and Burgess, eds., *The One Mediator, the Saints, and Mary*.
8. John 3:30.
9. 1 Corinthians 2:2.
10. Quoted in Forde, *On Being a Theologian of the Cross*, 77.

the cross to a theology of glory, which tries to get to God not through the gospel of the crucified Christ but through philosophy (reason), mysticism (religious exercises), or morality (good works). He said there are two ways of doing theology, the way of glory and the way of the cross. The way of glory rises up to meet God at the level of God in heaven; the way of the cross encounters God in the manger, in lowly things, in the suffering and death of the naked man who died on a hill outside the gate.

The cross of Christ is not simply the tragic fate of a human being, whose name is Jesus. The person dying on the cross is not a mere man; he is God in human flesh and blood. This event teaches those who wish to become theologians a new concept of God, so different from the myths of other gods in the pantheon of the world's religions. The great religions of the world teach that God cannot suffer, God cannot bleed, God cannot die. God has no feelings, God has no passions, God has nothing in common with the suffering and sorry lot of human beings, in sharing their anguish, despair, and sickness unto death. Theologians of glory think that what happened to Jesus affected only his human nature, so eager are they to exempt God of deprivation and degradation. For Paul the apostle and Luther the Reformer what happened on the cross happened to God. Theologians of glory flee from the crucified God in favor of the omnipotent God of majesty. Ashamed to find God on the cross of Christ, they rather climb a ladder to heaven, trusting in their human potential, peak experiences, or superior reason.

Luther was bold to say, "If it is not true that God died for us, but only a man died, we are lost. . . . So that it could be said: God died, God suffered, God bled. According to his nature God cannot die, but since God and man are united in the one person of Jesus, it is correct to talk about God's death when that man dies who is one person with God."[11] Four hundred-fifty years later, Dietrich Bonhoeffer, the martyr who died on Hitler's scaffold, said the same thing: "God allows himself to be edged out of the world onto the cross. God is weak and powerless in the world, and that is exactly the way, the only way, in which he can be with us and help us. . . . Only a suffering God can help."[12] Luther and Bonhoeffer were rephrasing Paul, who wrote, "Who though he was in the form of God . . .

---

11. Cited in the "Formula of Concord, Solid Declaration, Article VII, The Person of Christ," 599.
12. Bonhoeffer, *Letters and Papers from Prison*, 220.

he humbled himself and became obedient unto death, even death on a cross."[13] Only in Christianity do we find this idea that God and the gallows go together. Luther underscored the idea that we should not speculate about the unfathomable mysteries of God in his majesty; we should rather focus all our attention on God on the cross.

Theories of the Atonement

The Christian tradition has developed a number of theories of atonement to answer the question of what Christ's death on the cross accomplished for the salvation of humanity. We can distinguish four different theories and offer a thumbnail sketch of each.

The ransom theory of the atonement goes back to the ancient church, was taught by foremost theologians such as Origen of Alexandria, St. Gregory of Nyssa, and St. Augustine of Hippo. It became traditional church teaching for a thousand years until St. Anselm of Canterbury replaced it with his satisfaction theory. The ransom theory teaches that the death of Christ was a ransom that God had to pay to the devil because since the fall of Adam and Eve he held all their progeny captive. The devil accepted the ransom, not knowing that the cross was a trap and the blood of Christ the bait. The devil could have no claim on Christ who was without sin and God incognito. Justice was done and God was able to set humans free from the devil's clutch.

As a theory it could claim to be based on several passages of Scripture. "The Son of man came not to be served but to serve, and to give his life as a ransom for many."[14] And, "For there is one God, and there is one mediator between God and men, the man Christ Jesus, who gave himself as a ransom for all."[15] The ransom motif is not itself objectionable. St. Anselm and many others, however, have criticized the idea that a ransom had to be paid to the devil—himself being a rebel and enemy of God—because the devil isn't owed anything and so has no rightful claim against human beings. Others reject the ransom theory because it suggests that God is in debt to the devil and in the transaction acts as a trickster. The Scripture passages do not say

13. Philippians 2:6a, 8.
14. Matthew 20:28 and Mark 10:45.
15. 1 Timothy 2:5–6.

to whom the ransom is paid. The point that makes gospel sense is that the ransom sets humanity free from bondage to sin, death, and the devil.

The satisfaction theory was formulated by St. Anselm of Canterbury in his classic writing *Cur Deus Homo?*[16] This theory is most widely accepted by Roman Catholics and conservative Evangelicals. Anselm's bedrock principle was the justice of God. He defined sin as an affront to God's justice, as refusal to honor him. Therefore, sinners are indebted to God. Those who refuse to obey and honor God withhold what is owed to him. That is sin. That leaves two options. Either sinners must be punished or satisfaction must somehow be made. Punishment does not satisfy God because he wills eternal happiness for all. So satisfaction is the only viable alternative. However, human beings are not able to provide the satisfaction because they are stuck in their sins. So how can satisfaction be made? Only man is required to make this satisfaction. But only God is able to do so. Humans owe the debt but are not able to pay it. Only God can pay it, but he does not owe it. The wonder of the gospel is that Jesus Christ is both God and man. Only he, the God-man, can do what is necessary, bear the guilt of human sin and pay the debt required.

The theory is airtight. The problem is that in the satisfaction theory the justice of God preempts the love of God. Why would a loving God require the death of his Son to compensate for the collective sins of humanity? Why is justice given the last word?

The moral influence theory places the greatest stress not on the justice of God but on the love of God. The loving sacrifice of Jesus on the cross inspires hearts and minds and moves them to obedience, love, and trust in Christ. This was Peter Abelard's (1079–1142) proposal contra Anselm, the author of the satisfaction theory. This view became popular in modern liberal Protestantism, allergic to ideas of punishments and satisfactions for sins committed against the honor and justice of God. Jesus is seen, rather, as the perfect example, a hero of religion, but not more than a man. What can he do for those who are enslaved to sin but influence them to moral striving by his good example? This view does not take human sin seriously nor the judgment of a righteous God. It fails the biblical test by every measure.

---

16. Translation: Why Did God Become Man?

The traditional three theories of the atonement were superseded by a fourth view proposed by Gustaf Aulén, author of a book entitled *Christus Victor*.[17] He did not reject the motives of the three theories, but he aimed to reaffirm the strong biblical motif of the victory of Christ over the demonic powers that hold people in bondage. The biblical passage Aulén quoted most frequently was, "God was in Christ reconciling the world to himself."[18] What he saw in this verse was that God from beginning to end was in Christ gaining a victory over the demonic powers that held people in bondage. God is the reconciler and the reconciled. The important thing is that it does not happen subjectively in humans, but happens objectively in God's relationship to the world. God in Christ is the victor over the powers of evil—sin, guilt, death, the devil, the law—inimical to God that hold people in bondage. This is the gospel of God redeeming and reconciling the world unto himself.

Descent Into Hell

The Apostles' Creed states that after Jesus died, "he descended into hell." Between Jesus' death on the cross on Good Friday and his resurrection from the tomb on Easter Sunday, he spent Holy Saturday in hell, known as sheol in Hebrew and hades in Greek. There is no New Testament basis for this expression in the Apostles' Creed and scholars cannot find any precedent in Christian teaching before the third century. In the Old Testament sheol has two compartments for the departed souls, one for the wicked and one for the righteous. The wicked souls are in a place of anguish and torment and the righteous are in Abraham's bosom, a place of peace and quiet.

Where was Jesus on Holy Saturday? On the cross Jesus said to the penitent thief on his side, "Today you will be with me in Paradise."[19] It is likely that paradise is Abraham's bosom, where righteous persons go after they die. In any case Jesus descended into hell or hades and there he liberated the Old Testament saints of old, patriarchs and prophets. First Peter 3:19 says that Jesus, after he was put to death, "went and preached to the spirits in prison." This passage has given rise to speculation that Jesus preached to all those who died without having had a chance to hear the gospel, not

17. Aulén, *Christus Victor*.
18. 2 Corinthians 5:19.
19. Luke 23:43.

only Old Testament saints but people everywhere in the world of other religions or no religion at all.

Tradition is divided as to whether Jesus' descent into hell was the extremity of his humiliation or the beginning of his exaltation. If his descent meant a continuation of his state of humiliation, he would still experience suffering as the penalty for human sin. But on the cross Jesus declared, "It is finished." His atoning death is completed. His descent into hell is a triumph. Holy Saturday is liturgically commemorated as the "harrowing of hell." To harrow means to despoil, to violate, to liberate the righteous held captive by Satan. This view is more in keeping with the good news of Christ's triumphant victory over sin, death, and the devil.

The Resurrection

The idea of a person being raised from the dead came out of the experience of the Jewish people during their exile in Babylon, somewhere in today's Iraq. The faith of the Jewish people was put to the test. They struggled with the question of whether God had forgotten them, especially all those faithful ones who died under pagan rule and domination. Had they believed and trusted God in vain? Would Israel perish forever in enemy territory, with no hope for the future? Then the prophet Ezekiel had a vision, the vision of the Valley of Dry Bones, made famous in two popular folk songs, one sung by Woody Guthrie, "Ezekiel Saw the Wheel," and one by Fred Waring, "Dem Bones." The dry bones will live again; they will put on flesh and sinews, covered with skin, and begin to breathe again. The vision of resurrection was born of hope, hope for Israel beyond the exile, hope for restoration to the land of promise. Those who died in captivity, loyal to Yahweh and his Torah, would arise from their graves to share in the return to Palestine. The righteous ones who were killed by their slave masters are presently safe in the arms of God and at last will be raised to share in the blessings of the age to come.

Christianity began as a messianic movement and took over the Jewish belief in resurrection. In Jesus' time the resurrection was a disputed belief; the Sadducees said there is no resurrection, but the Pharisees accepted it.[20] The first believers in Jesus as the Messiah were all Jews. No matter how much

20. Acts 23:8.

they disagreed on such things as observing the Torah, Jewish food laws, the rite of circumcision, and keeping the Sabbath, the first followers of Jesus all believed he was raised from the dead, the chief point of difference from their Jewish brothers and sisters. But in believing in Jesus' resurrection they did not think that constituted a break with their Hebrew faith. They were all Jews believing in Jesus as the risen Messiah, Lord and Savior. They knew there was something different about Jesus. He was in serious conflict with the Jewish leaders of his time, daring to challenge aspects of the Torah and claiming greater authority for himself. He would frequently say, "You have heard it said; but I say unto you."

The parting of the ways between Jews who followed Jesus and those who did not had to do not with belief in the resurrection as such but in believing that Jesus was the Messiah that Jews had longed and prayed for since their time in exile. The double ending of Jesus, his cross and resurrection, was the watershed, the crucial point of transition from Judaism to Christianity. Even today Jews can accept Jesus' teachings and exemplary life and many do, but when they interpret his death and resurrection as revelatory of his messianic identity, they are *eo ipso* Christians.[21]

Pinchas Lapide is an orthodox Jewish theologian who has published a series of dialogues with Christian theologians, including Jürgen Moltmann, Wolfhart Pannenberg, Hans Küng, and Peter Stuhlmacher. In these dialogues he has reclaimed the Jewishness of Jesus, of the first Christians, and of the New Testament in general. He sees no good reason to deny the New Testament accounts of the resurrection of Jesus, as well as no good reason to believe in the Messiahship of Jesus. He offers a Jewish argument. Traditionally Jews believed that when the Messiah comes, he will bring in the kingdom of God that will utterly change things for the better in a dramatic way. Look out the window, he suggests, and you will see that the world remains the same, given all the genocide, racism, violence, wars, nuclear threat, poverty, hunger—the list is endless. When the Messiah comes, Jews believed, the reign of God will inaugurate an era of peace, righteousness, and fulfillment for all, starting with those on the bottom. If the resurrection of Jesus happened as a historical event, and Lapide believes it did, it is obvious that the world is still mired in the same old sins and evil, proving that

---

21. See Lapide, *The Resurrection of Jesus*.

the messianic age has not yet arrived. Jesus is risen, Lapide says, but that's no proof he is the Messiah.

The first Christians, all Jews, believed both that Jesus is risen and that he is the Messiah. Why? That's the question they had to answer, and every generation of Christians thereafter. The disciples, friends, and followers of Jesus were scared, shattered, and scattered late Good Friday afternoon when their teacher died on the cross. Then Easter Sunday came. What a turnabout. One day they felt ashamed for having denied and betrayed their leader. In a matter of days they embarked on a revolutionary mission to preach the gospel to all the nations. They were filled with joy, hope, and confidence because Jesus was alive, in spite of having to suffer torture, persecution, and martyrdom for their witness to their crucified Messiah and risen Lord. Ever since there has been and there can be no true Christian faith without sharing the belief of the apostles and first missionaries that Jesus is risen. Without this faith there is nothing unique to declare to the nations that other religions cannot provide equally well. The Apostle Paul said it first: "If Christ has not been raised, then our proclamation has been in vain and your faith has been in vain. . . . If Christ has not been raised, your faith is futile and you are still in your sins. . . . If for this life only we have hoped in Christ, we are of all people most to be pitied."[22]

Paul's punctilious assertion captures the overwhelming consensus among churches of every nation through the centuries despite the sad naysaying of some contemporary liberal Protestant theologians. Here are but a few examples among scores that could be quoted. A. J. M. Wedderburn writes that "Paul's logic simply cannot hold water today. His rhetoric has led him astray."[23] Robert Funk tells about how he once formulated the proposition that the resurrection was an event in the life of Jesus, then presented it to members of the Jesus Seminar. Then he wrote, "My proposition was received with hilarity by several Fellows. One suggested that it was an oxymoron. . . . Others alleged that the formulation was meaningless, since we all assume that Jesus' life ended with his crucifixion and death. . . . After all, John Dominic Crossan has confessed, 'I do not think that anyone, anywhere, at any time brings dead people back to life.'"[24] Schubert Ogden confessed that

---

22. 1 Corinthians 15:14, 17, 19.
23. Wedderburn, *Beyond Resurrection*, 154.
24. Funk, *Honest to Jesus*, 258.

the resurrection of Jesus "would be just as relevant to my salvation as an existing self or person as that the carpenter next door just drove a nail into a two-by-four, or that American technicians have at last been successful in recovering a nose cone that had first been placed in orbit around the earth."[25] David Griffin, penning a sentiment polar opposite to that of the Apostle Paul's, wrote, "Christian faith as I understand it is possible apart from belief in Jesus' resurrection in particular and life beyond bodily death in general, and because of the widespread skepticism regarding these traditional beliefs, they should be presented as optional."[26] Rudolf Bultmann concluded, after demythologizing the New Testament gospel, "An historical fact which involves a resurrection from the dead is utterly inconceivable."[27]

The church stands and falls with belief in the resurrection of Jesus. Strictly from a critical historical point of view, without any recourse to faith or doctrine, it can safely be said that there would have been no Christianity without it. Two centuries ago, David Friedrich Strauss, after dissolving the entire life of Jesus, from the incarnation to the resurrection, into a Christ myth,[28] asked the question, "Can we still be Christians?" He resoundingly answered, "No!" The old faith of traditional Christians and the new faith of enlightened moderns are contradictory. Not all scholars are equally honest. Gerd Lüdemann, German New Testament theologian, wrote a book on the resurrection,[29] in which he argued that though we modern people are incapable of believing that the resurrection of Jesus really happened, we can still be Christian. We can still affirm the moral teachings and exemplary life of the historical Jesus. A few years later Gerd Lüdemann reconsidered and renounced the Christian faith, admitting there's no point in calling oneself a Christian if one does not believe that God raised Jesus from the dead.

The resurrection is more than a resuscitation of the physical body of Jesus. Lazarus was resuscitated; he was not resurrected because he had to die again. His return to life did not transcend the conditions of his mortal existence. Jesus was bodily resurrected, but it was a new kind of body. St. Paul said

25. Ogden, *Christ Without Myth*, 136.
26. Griffin, *A Process Christology*, 12.
27. Bultmann, "The New Testament and Mythology," 1, 41.
28. Strauss, *The Life of Jesus Critically Examined*.
29. Lüdemann, *The Resurrection of Jesus*.

it was a spiritual body, a *soma pneumatikos*.[30] The earthly mortal body is transformed into an immortal spiritual body. Christ's spiritual body incorporates the entire community of members through baptism into his death and resurrection. God transformed the risen Jesus into a new mode of being that includes his church. The church is the risen body of Christ.

The early Christians did not come to believe in the risen Jesus by their own reason and strength. We today believe because we trust the testimonies of the first witnesses and believers. This is not merely our own doing. The Holy Spirit made the reality of the resurrected Christ present in the life of each believer and the whole community of faith. Paul wrote: "If the Spirit of him who raised Jesus from the dead dwells in you, he who raised Christ from the dead will give life to your mortal bodies also through his Spirit who dwells in you."[31] The Spirit's work is to make Christ really present and to apply his benefits through the preaching of the gospel and the administration of the sacraments.

The Ascension and Session at the Right Hand of the Father

The ascension of Jesus is part of the whole narrative of the Son of God descending from heaven, being born of a virgin, living a human life, crucified on a cross, raised from the grave, and after forty days appearing now and then to his friends and followers, then ascended to heaven and still sits at the right hand of his Father. These two pieces of the Creed, "He ascended into heaven and sits at the right hand of the Father," have been much neglected in the church, and not only in the church's worship but in theology. There are several plausible reasons for this. The ascension took place on a weekday and so tends to get little recognition in Sunday worship services. Another factor is that Luke is the only one to tell the story of the ascension. It is not mentioned by Paul, Matthew, Mark, John, or anywhere else in Scripture. The New Testament does not itself explain the existential (soteriological) relevance of Jesus ascending to heaven and sitting at the right hand of God the Father. In addition Jesus' departure to heaven, leaving his disciples behind

---

30. 1 Corinthians 15:44.
31. Romans 8:11.

on earth, seems to contradict Jesus' assurance in the very last verse of Matthew, "Lo, I am with you always, to the close of the age."[32]

The story of the ascension also became an issue in the Lord's Supper controversy between Martin Luther and Huldreich Zwingli (Marburg Colloquy, 1529). Zwingli took the story literally. If Jesus was physically taken up into heaven and sits at God's right hand, this proves he is not really present as the host of the sacred meal. Everyone knows that no human being can be in more than one place at a time. This was supposed to clinch the argument against Luther's sacramental teaching that Christ is really present in body and blood in, with, and under the material elements of bread and wine. When Jesus said at the Last Supper, "This is my body," Zwingli said that the word "is" meant "figuratively." Luther objected; it was meant literally. But to interpret the phrase "at God's right hand" literally is a childish notion. Symbolically it refers to the power of God by which Christ can be everywhere present, as he said, "All power has been given to me in heaven and on earth."[33]

To the question, "Where did Jesus go on Ascension Day?" Karl Barth said the ascension is the story of the homecoming of the Son of Man who had wandered into a far country, a homecoming to the Father's house. After suffering a terrible unjust humiliation Jesus was exalted to a glorious reunion with his Father. He is lifted up on high to a position of power, rulership, and honor. Luther said, the "right hand" is a symbol of power, exercised in the name of the highest ruler. If Jesus is at the right hand of God Almighty, he is now in charge. He rules by divine right. As the popular American spiritual says, "He's got the whole world in his hands." That is a statement of faith, contrary to all appearances. The ascended Christ has the right and power to rule in the church according to his grace and gospel through the Word and Sacraments. There can be no other ultimate ruler in the church, and every impostor who has tried has been dubbed the Antichrist.

Jesus' session at the right hand of the Father means that he is also active beyond the walls of the church. His claim to Lordship reaches the outer circumference of creation, touching everything that lives and moves in nature and creation. "All things were made through him, and without him was

---

32. Matthew 28:20.
33. Matthew 28:18.

not anything made that was made."[34] All things were made by him and find their ultimate meaning and goal in him." Paul in his letter to the Colossians affirmed this truth most eloquently:

> He is the image of the invisible God, the first-born of all creation; for in him all things were created, in heaven and on earth, visible and invisible, whether thrones or dominions or principalities or authorities—all things were created through him and for him. He is before all things, and in him all things hold together. He is the head of the body, the church; he is the beginning, the first-born from the dead, so that he might come to have first place in everything. For in him was all the fullness of God pleased to dwell, and through him to reconcile to himself all things, whether on earth or in heaven, making peace by the blood of his cross.[35]

How could Paul say these things, living as he was as a Roman citizen under the imperial rule of Almighty Caesar? Martin Niemöller preached a sermon in Berlin announcing the same thing under the heinous dictatorship of *Der Führer*, Adolf Hitler, "Jesus is *Führer!*" All the pretentious rulers of world history are far beneath the throne to which Jesus has been raised to the position of glory, power, and dominion. All the superpowers directing nations, all the world rulers in charge of empires, political, economic, social, national, and international—all of these puffed up hierarchies are no match for the Lordship of Christ who sits at the right hand of the Father. This is what Paul encourages preachers to preach and the faithful to believe celebrating the ascension of Jesus to the right hand of the Father.

The Return of Christ

The Lordship of Christ in world history is hidden, even from the eyes of faith. The power he exercises at the right hand of God is not apparent. It never makes the "breaking news." Suffering and war and crime continue unabated. The world is still writhing in the grip of evil forces. No wonder the saints have cried out, "How long, O Lord!" How long will it be before you take charge and show the world your righteous power? No one can answer that, but believers are buoyed up by the promise that Christ will come again with glory to judge the living and the dead according to his justice and love. At last his kingdom shall have no end; he shall reign

34. John 1:3.
35. Colossians 1:15–20.

for ever and ever! With these thoughts we are entering the province of eschatology, the doctrine of the last things, the resurrection of the dead and the life everlasting.

Questions for Discussion

1. What is a myth? Are New Testament scholars right in speaking of myth in the New Testament?
2. The Gospels narrate that Jesus was born of the Virgin Mary. Christian theology speaks of his pre-existence. Is this a logical paradox, a mystery of faith, a confusion of categories, or what?
3. The Gospels speak of Jesus having siblings, brothers and sisters. Yet, the Christian tradition maintains, in seeming contradiction, that Mary remained always a virgin (*semper virgine*). Reflect on what difference it makes.
4. In his *Heidelberg Disputation* Martin Luther contrasted two types of theology, a theology of the cross and a theology of glory. What are some of the basic features of such a contrast?
5. In the history of Christian doctrine theologians have offered various explanations of the meaning of Jesus' death on the cross. Name them and discuss the merits of each one.
6. What is the salvific meaning of confessing that Jesus descended into hell (hades or Gehenna)?
7. Did Jesus really rise from the dead? This is the teaching of the New Testament as well as of the major creeds and confessions of classical Christianity. Yet, some modern liberal Protestant theologians say this belief is unintelligible, unbelievable, and should therefore remain optional for Christians today. What do you think?

8. The Holy Spirit

It is unfortunate that the Holy Spirit has been the subject of so much controversy in the history of Christianity. Jesus promised his disciples on his last days on earth, "The Counselor, the Holy Spirit, whom the Father will send in my name, he will teach you all things, and bring to your remembrance all that I have said to you. Peace I leave with you; my peace I give to you; not as the world gives do I give to you. Let not your hearts be troubled; neither let them be afraid."[1] The Holy Spirit is the personal agency of God to bestow life, unity, peace, harmony, hope, and love in the assemblies of those who believe in Jesus Christ as their Lord and Savior. We must leave it to textbooks on church history to tell the story of Tertullian and Montanism. Montanus (second century) declared that the Holy Spirit was giving new revelations to the church, a movement called the "New Prophecy." Tertullian (160–230), theologian from Carthage, North Africa, and known as the father of ecclesiastical Latin, provided precise language for the orthodox doctrines of the Trinity and Christology. He joined the prophetic sectarian Montanist movement, which was condemned as heretical by Rome, and for this reason, despite Tertullian's enormous contribution to orthodox theology, he was never declared a saint.

Controversies About the Holy Spirit

The Holy Spirit was also the subject of controversy that contributed to the split between Eastern Orthodoxy and Western Catholicism in 1054 AD that has not yet been overcome. The controversy concerned the Latin term, *filioque*, which means "and from the Son." The term was not included in the Nicene Creed of 325 AD or in its sequel of 381 AD, the Nicene-Constantinopolitan Creed. They simply said that the Holy Spirit "proceeds from the Father." But in 589 AD the word "*filioque*" was added at a council in Spain,

---

1. John 14:26–27.

without consent of the Eastern Orthodox Church, to read "The Holy Spirit proceeds from the Father and the Son." The theological question is: Does the Holy Spirit proceed only from the Father or from both the Father and the Son? And what differences does it make? The ecclesiological question is: What right does any church authority have to unilaterally change the wording of a creed adopted by an ecumenical council?

Joachim, Abbot of Fiore (twelfth century), taught that the Trinity refers to three periods of salvation history. His apocalyptic ideas were based on his exposition of the book of Revelation.[2] The first is the time of the Father in the Old Testament, the second is the time of the Son in the New Testament still continuing in the life of the church, and the third is the time of the Holy Spirit that in the future will bring about a revolutionary transformation of the church. He calls this an *ecclesia spiritualis*. In this spiritual church Christians will reach a state of moral perfection and sinlessness. In this new fellowship of the Spirit there will no longer be a need for the organized church, its hierarchy, its bishops, including the pope, and such things as sacraments, liturgical worship, as well as creeds and dogma. The visible church with its priests will give way to a monastic order in which all shall live as holy monks. The New Testament, having achieved its purpose, will be replaced by an unwritten "eternal gospel" prophesied in Revelation 14:6. Joachim calculated that the third age of the Spirit would commence in the year 1260. For Joachim Christ and the church are signs of the future but not the future itself. They will be superseded by the future unfolding of the Holy Spirit in history. The transition from the second age of the Son to the third age of the Spirit will entail the dying of the institutional church to make way for a spiritual kingdom of peace and concord, universal love, freedom, and fulfillment of all humanity. Nothing remarkable happened in the year 1260 AD. This was not the first or the last utopian dream shattered on the reefs of reality, by a misguided interpretation of the Holy Spirit of God the Father and his Son Jesus Christ.

At the time of the Reformation Martin Luther became embroiled in a controversy with a dissident group of spiritualists he described by the word *Schwärmerei*. In his view they were "fanatics," because they believed the Holy Spirit spoke to them directly through unmediated internal experience.

---

2. For an extensive discussion of Joachim's ideas, see Polak, *The Image of the Future*, 178–83.

For Luther God works through the external means of the preached word of the gospel and the holy sacraments of the church.

The gifts of the Spirit that the Apostle Paul wrote about became controversial in the twentieth century in response to the charismatic movement. Paul identified nine spiritual gifts: wisdom, knowledge, faith, healing, miracles, prophecy, discernment of spirits, speaking in tongues, and interpretation of tongues.[3] These gifts are distributed variously to individuals for the purpose of "building up" and "for edification" of the church, the body of Christ.[4] Pentecostals and charismatics in various other denominations believe that the gifts of the Spirit are still available to contemporary Christians by the infilling of the Spirit, by Spirit baptism. When Christianity became the established church with state approval in the Roman Empire, the miraculous gifts seemed to cease, except perhaps among fringe and cultic groups. Cessationism is the view that maintains that the gifts of prophecy, healing miracles, and speaking in tongues ceased with the death of the apostles. By the second century there is scarcely any mention of them in the writings of the church fathers. The jury is still out, theologically speaking, whether cessationism or non-cessationism or some modified position in between is right. The old adage may be apropos: "not one size fits all." The gifts may have ceased wherever and whenever Christianity became established, secularized, hearts grew cold, and the flames of the Spirit flickered. Ecumenical dogmatics is wise to heed the counsel of Gamaliel, a Pharisee and teacher of the law, weighing in on the fate of the apostles accused of teaching in the name of Jesus: "Men of Israel, take care what you do with these men. . . . So in the present case I tell you, keep away from these men and let them alone; for if this plan or this undertaking is of men, it will fail; but if it is of God, you will not be able to overthrow them. You might even be found opposing God."[5] Pentecostalism is spreading around the world at a rapid rate, especially in the Global South, unsurpassed by any other missionary evangelistic movements.

The doctrine of the Holy Spirit also became a controversial issue at the Third Assembly of the World Council of Churches in New Delhi, India, 1961. The meeting produced a statement on church unity. One of the

3. 1 Corinthians 12:4–10.
4. 1 Corinthians 14:12 and 26.
5. Acts 5:34–35 and 38–39.

speakers, however, looked beyond unity among churches and asked about unity among the major world religions. The speaker offered a proposal. Since faith in Christ is peculiar only to Christians and is thus the major point of difference between Christianity and other religions, focus on the Spirit would be more promising in the search for common ground. The idea met with a strong rebuke from Orthodox participants, in spite of their opposition to the *filioque* clause. They were opposed to separating the Spirit from Christ or to suggest that there is a way to the Father not mediated by Christ. In orthodox trinitarian theology the work of the Spirit cannot be separated from the work of the Son. The ancient trinitarian rule is, "the works of the Trinity are undivided."[6] Any spirit separated from the person and work of Christ is other than the Holy Spirit who proceeds from the Father. One of the last things Jesus said to his disciples was: "When the Counselor comes, whom I will send to you from the Father, even the Spirit of truth, who proceeds from the Father, he will bear witness to me. . . . It is to your advantage that I go away, for if I do not go away, the Counselor will not come to you; but if I go, I will send him to you."[7]

The Person and Work of the Holy Spirit

The above series of controversies indicate that every misinterpretation of the person and work of the Holy Spirit leads to a serious distortion of the gospel of Jesus Christ. The first question to answer is, "Who is the Holy Spirit?" The Holy Spirit is a real person in whose name believers in Christ are baptized, along with the name of the Father and the name of the Son. He is the third member of the triune God, equal in every way with the Father and the Son. In the New Testament he is first named in the Gospel accounts of Jesus' birth. The Apostles' Creed confesses that Jesus, God's only Son, was conceived by the Holy Spirit and born of the virgin Mary—taken almost word for word from the first chapters of the Gospels of Matthew and Luke. In the Old Testament the Spirit was active at the beginning of creation: "The earth was without form and void, and darkness was upon the face of the deep; and the Spirit of God was moving over the face of the waters."[8] The Nicene Creed confesses that the Holy Spirit is "the giver of life," not

---

6. *Opera trinitatis indivisa sunt.*

7. John 15:26 and 16:7.

8. Genesis 1:2. From Hebrew *ruach* is translated as "spirit," the same word for wind or breath.

8. THE HOLY SPIRIT

only the new spiritual life of believers and the Christian community, but all of life in the whole created universe.

When Jesus was baptized by John at the river Jordan, he heard his Father in heaven saying, "This is my beloved Son," and at the same time he saw the Spirit of God descending like a dove on him—three members of the Trinity in one scene.[9]

The Spirit is the mediator between the saving work of Christ and the community of faith. He internalizes the love of God and the forgiveness of sins in the hearts of those who hear his truthful testimony to Christ. "The Counselor, the Holy Spirit, whom the Father will send in my name, he will teach you all things, and bring to your remembrance all that I have said to you."[10] "When the Spirit of truth comes, he will guide you into all the truth; for he will not speak on his own authority, but whatever he hears he will speak."[11] The Spirit is God taking up residence within the person who believes in Jesus, bearing fruits fit for the kingdom of God, such as love, joy, peace, patience, kindness, goodness, faithfulness, gentleness, and self-control.[12] Showing forth these virtues in daily life is what Paul means to "walk by the Spirit."[13] The Holy Spirit is on our side *creating* our relationship to God, opening our hearts and minds to receive everything the Father wills to give us through his Son.[14]

The Holy Spirit is the effective communicator of the Word of God, the written word of the Holy Scriptures, and the preached Word from the age of the apostles to the present. "All scripture is inspired by God and profitable for teaching, for reproof, for correction, and for training in righteousness."[15] The Holy Spirit did not only inspire the patriarchs and prophets of the Old Testament but also empowered the evangelists and apostles of the New

---

9. Matthew 3:16.
10. John 14:26.
11. John 16:13.
12. Galatians 5:22–23.
13. Galatians 5:16.
14. Martin Luther has often been criticized for being too christocentric and weak on the Holy Spirit. Regin Prenter answered such criticism with his book on Luther's doctrine of the Holy Spirit, entitled *Spiritus Creator*.
15. 2 Timothy 3:16.

Testament to preach the gospel. "But you shall receive power when the Holy Spirit comes upon you; and you shall be my witnesses in Jerusalem, and in all Judea and Samaria and to the end of the earth."[16] Without the inspiration of the Spirit the Bible is merely a collection of ancient texts and not the canon of Holy Scripture, the book that belongs to the church in a special way. Without the Spirit the gospel is just an ancient myth no more true than any other, Babylonian or gnostic. Without the Spirit the church is merely another society with rules of membership dedicated to promote their own interests in the world. Without the Spirit the water of baptism is merely water, the wine and bread at the Lord's Supper do not convey the body and blood of Christ. Only those born of the Spirit enter into the kingdom of God. It is not enough to say, "Lord, Lord." A true confession of Jesus as Lord is only possible through the Holy Spirit. Faith is a gift of the Holy Spirit. This is the beginning of the "Christian Life," the life justified by the grace of God alone (*sola gratia*), on account of Christ alone (*solus Christus*), through faith alone (*sola fide*), apart from having to satisfy the rigorous requirements of the law.

In his *Small Catechism* Luther wrote an explanation to the Third Article of the Apostles' Creed that sums up what the New Testament says about the regenerating and sanctifying role of the Holy Spirit in making Christians. At the same time it sums up what all Christian churches believe and teach concerning the work of the Holy Spirit.

> I believe that by my own understanding or strength I cannot believe in Jesus Christ or come to him, but instead the Holy Spirit has called me through the gospel, enlightened me with his gifts, made me holy and kept me in the true faith, just as he calls, gathers, enlightens, and makes holy the whole Christian church on earth and keeps it with Jesus Christ in the one common, truth faith. Daily in this Christian church the Holy Spirit abundantly forgives all sins—mine and those of all believers. On the last day the Holy Spirit will raise me and all the dead and will give to me and all believers in Christ eternal life. This is most certainly true.

---

16. Acts 1:8.

8. THE HOLY SPIRIT

Questions for Discussion

1. The Nicene Creed confesses that the Holy Spirit proceeds from the Father and the Son (*filioque*). Eastern Orthodoxy does not accept the "*filioque*." Why not? What theological difference does it make, in your view?

2. How did Joachim of Fiore understand the Trinity, and the role of the Holy Spirit in particular?

3. At the time of the Reformation Luther was involved in a controversy over the work of the Holy Spirit. Describe the controversy, and do you think the controversy has any present-day relevance?

4. A controversy occurred in the early church whether the charismatic gifts of the Spirit ceased with the death of the last apostles, or whether they are meant to continue in the church to this day. How would you resolve this controversy, which is still alive within Christianity worldwide, theologically?

5. Why has it been difficult to think of the Holy Spirit as a Person, equal in every respect with the Father and the Son?

6. The belief that the writers of the Bible were inspired by the Holy Spirit has been invoked to prove its inerrancy. Does the authority of the Bible depend on the theory that there are no errors of any kind in the Bible?

7. What was Luther's explanation of the Third Article of the Apostles' Creed regarding the soteriological role of the Holy Spirit?

9. The Church

The right starting point for constructing the Christian doctrine of the church is Jesus' proclamation of the gospel of the kingdom of God. Alfred Loisy (1857–1940), the founder of biblical modernism in Roman Catholic theology, cynically quipped, "Jesus foretold the kingdom and it was the church that came."[1] Yet, that happens to be exactly true. The church is not the kingdom of God; nor was Jesus the founder of the church. Jesus was surrounded by his mother, family, disciples, friends, and followers but they were not the first church reported in the book of Acts. Pentecost was the birth date of the Christian church. The Holy Spirit created and motivated the first Christian assembly in Jerusalem, under the leadership of the twelve apostles. When the gospel spread from Jerusalem to Antioch, there "the disciples for the first time were called Christians."[2] They also called themselves "People of the Way." This was before the early church was equipped with the New Testament or a creed. They had their memory of the life and teachings of their Master and his promise that they would "receive power when the Holy Spirit has come upon you; and you shall be my witnesses."[3] The Holy Spirit is the personal active agent who connected the kingdom of God proleptically present in the ministry of Jesus with its new instantiations in the church of the apostles. The Holy Spirit is a down payment (earnest or guarantee)[4] of the eschatological kingdom that Jesus preached in the new community that he created. The Spirit who enabled Jesus to perform mighty acts—signs of the coming kingdom he announced—is the same Spirit who continued his miraculous works through the apostles gathered in the name of Jesus.

---

1. Loisy, *The Gospel and the Church*, 166.
2. Acts 11:26.
3. Acts 1:8.
4. 1 Corinthians 1:22; 5:5; Ephesians 1:14.

The Nature of the Church

The church is a many-splendored thing whose nature is depicted in many different images. In Roman Catholic theology the church has been called the "perfect society," (Vatican I), the "mystical body of Christ" (Johan Adam Möhler), the "People of God" (Vatican II), and the "sacrament of salvation" (Karl Rahner). Other images are favored in Eastern Orthodox theology, such as, "Icon of the Trinity" (Bruno Forte), the "eucharistic community" (Georges Florovsky), the "communion of churches" (John Zizioulas). The Apostles' Creed confesses that the "holy catholic church" is the "communion of saints." Martin Luther referred to the church as the "creature of the Word." For Jürgen Moltmann the church is the "messianic community" and for Wolfhart Pannenberg the "prolepsis of the kingdom." Feminist theologian Elizabeth Schüssler Fiorenza sees the early church as a "discipleship community of equals." A common metaphor for the church in modern ecumenical documents is the "pilgrim people of God." In Pauline theology the church is the "body of Christ." This is a strong image because it integrates the church into the person of Christ. The whole Christ includes both head and body (*totus Christus, caput et corpus*). Each of these images conveys an important aspect of the church.

The One, Holy, Catholic, and Apostolic Church

The modern ecumenical movement that began in the early years of the twentieth century encouraged all churches—sensing their lack of unity as a scandal, contradicting Christ's farewell prayer to his Father in behalf of his followers he was about to leave behind "that they may all be one, even as thou, Father, art in me, and I in thee, that they may also be in us"[5]—to give unprecedented attention to the doctrine of the church in the hope that they might discover a breakthrough to overcome their lamentable divisions. That quest for church unity is still going on with no breakthrough in sight. Yet, enormous progress has been made in the way ecumenically engaged churches understand the attributes and marks of the one, holy, catholic, and apostolic church.

All Christians confess the church of which they are members to be a part of the "one, holy, catholic, and apostolic church." The church of Christ is

5. John 17:21.

one; it is the body of Christ, and Christ cannot be divided. In spite of the fact that Christians belong to different denominations bearing names that reflect their distinctive histories, they are one by virtue of their faith in the one Lord, all baptized into the one mystical body of Christ, sanctified by the one and the same Holy Spirit, and united by a common faith, hope, and love. Pope John Paul II spoke for many when he said in his 1995 Encyclical Letter, *Ut Unum Sint*, that despite existing separations, "We all belong to Christ." Yet, the paradox remains that though Christians who belong to Christ are one, the church bodies of which they are members are still divided. While the churches remain separated, they need a new concept of unity that will break the present logjam in which each church tends to think of itself as the true church, in some cases the only true church. Roman Catholic and Eastern Orthodox Churches still remain divided and yet each declares itself to be the only true church, and some Protestant churches do the same. Professor Edmund Schlink, official Lutheran observer at the Second Vatican Council, wrote an essay about his experience, "After the Council,"[6] in which he offers some thoughts which all churches would do well to consider, inasmuch as none of them has a theological concept of church unity convincing to others.

Here is a brief summary of Schlink's ideas concerning church unity. Every member of the church believes that he or she belongs to the one, holy, catholic, and apostolic church. And every church believes that Christ and his Spirit are alive in it. Traditionally every church begins its thinking about the church with itself and then dialogues with other churches to see which of its elements are present or lacking. This ecclesiocentric way of proceeding means that every church thinks of itself as the center around which the other churches orbit as planets around the sun. Then Schlink writes, worth quoting in full:

> All Christians are certain that the church whose message brought them to faith . . . is the one, holy, catholic, and apostolic church. But the working of Christ is not restricted to this one church. He works in freedom without being bound by the borders of our churches. We cannot be content to measure other churches in respect to ourselves, but we have to take our starting point with Christ, by whom we are measured along with all churches. He is the sun around whom we, together with other churches, orbit as

---

6. Schlink, "After the Council."

> planets and from whom we receive light. A kind of Copernican revolution is necessary in ecclesiological thinking. . . . Although Christ desires the unity of all believers, he is working in separated churches. . . . This means that Christ will not permit every separation brought about by the churches to be a separation from him. Through the working of this same Lord a unity of the separated is kept intact, a unity into which their division does not penetrate and which is not dissolved by their division. Through the reception of the gifts of the same Christ there remains a unity, which is hidden under the divisions—hidden from the eyes of the churches and from the eyes of the world.[7]

Christ who is holy makes those who believe in him holy. Jesus said, "I consecrate myself for their sakes that they may be made holy by the truth."[8] Christians are visible in the world; they do not look holy. Some who lived sanctified lives before they died have been consecrated as saints. In common parlance we hear about St. Paul, St. John, St. Irenaeus, St. Augustine, St. Thomas, St. Francis, but not St. Luther, St. Calvin, St. Wesley, or St. Knox. According to the New Testament all Christians are called "saints." It was customary for the Apostle Paul to address his letters, "To all the saints." Yet, he was the first to confess that "all are sinners."[9] From the New Testament point of view, all baptized and believing Christians are "saints and sinners" at the same time. Nor is it the case that the more one is a saint, the less one is a sinner. Karl Rahner said it well: "We are a church of sinners!" There is no church without "spot or wrinkle."[10] The Westminster Confession states, "The purest churches under heaven are subject to misuse and error." In his commentary on Paul's Epistle to the Romans, Luther wrote: "The saints in being righteous are at the same time sinners; they are righteous because they believe in Christ whose righteousness covers them and is imputed to them, but they are sinners because they do not fulfill the law and are not without sinful desires."[11] In an age of non-stop news and investigative reporting, it is impossible to be ignorant of the sinfulness of the church, and that goes for all churches. It is counter-intuitive to believe in the holiness of the church. But that is the point. The holiness of the church is a matter of faith, not sight.

---

7. Schlink, "After the Council," 526, 527, 528.
8. John 17:19 (Phillips Translation).
9. Romans 3:23.
10. Ephesians 5:27.
11. The Latin phrase for Luther's interpretation of Paul is *"simui iustus et peccator."*

The church possesses the attribute of holiness solely on account of Christ who imparts his righteousness to its sinful members.

Catholic is a word from the Greek *kath' ölon*, meaning according to the whole or universal. The catholic church refers to the whole body of believers who share the same faith in Christ and the same gospel. It is not restricted to a certain polity, administration, or regional identity; it refers to Christians and communities within all nations, languages, and ethnicities spread over the entire earth. The church is catholic with respect to geography, referring to the whole world in space; the church is also catholic with respect to temporality, referring to the time the church began to the end of time. Vincent of Lérins, a fifth-century theologian, wrote what is called the Vincentian Canon, to express what is "catholic" in terms of faith and doctrine. Catholic is "that faith which has been believed everywhere, always, and by all."[12] Vincent had in mind the undivided church founded by Christ and the apostles, and intended his Canon to distinguish what is orthodox teaching from heresies.

The confession that the church is apostolic means that it was founded on the faith and doctrines the apostles expressed in their writings and teachings.[13] Jesus said, "I will build my church."[14] He founded it on the apostles and promised the Counselor, the Holy Spirit, to guide and empower them. Some churches adopt the word *apostolic* as a name to distinguish their organization from other mainline churches. For them to be "apostolic" is to continue to practice the charismatic gifts of the Spirit such as speaking in tongues, healing, Spirit-baptism, prophecy, and so forth. This is not what "apostolic" means in the Nicene Creed, since by the fourth century the so-called "gifts of the Spirit" had ceased for the most part. A church is apostolic when it remains faithful to the tradition (*paradosis*) of the apostles, when it continues to preach (*kerygma*) and teach (*didache*) according to the witness (*martyria*) of the apostles. The church is apostolic when it gathers as a fellowship (*koinonia*) of believers for weekly worship (*leiturgia*) on the Lord's Day.

12. In Latin: "*Quod ubique, quod semper, quod ab omnibus creditum est.*" *The Commentary*, chapter 2.
13. Ephesians 2:19–20: "So then you are no longer strangers and sojourners, but you are fellow citizens with the saints and members of the household of God, built upon the foundation of the apostles and prophets, Christ Jesus himself being the chief cornerstone."
14. Matthew 16:18.

9. THE CHURCH

To recite the sentence in the Nicene Creed, "We believe in the one holy catholic and apostolic church" is one thing and surely important, but to find and join a church or a congregation that exhibits such attributes is something else and essential for every Christian person and family. Since ancient times theologians have attempted to answer the question of how to tell a true church from a false church. Church fathers such as Irenaeus, Tertullian, and Hippolytus were vehemently opposed to the heresy of gnosticism. The gnostic churches rejected the Old Testament; they separated the God of creation from the God of redemption; they rejected the law of Moses in favor of the gospel of Christ. They juxtaposed the freedom of the gospel to bondage under the law. There were heretical churches in the first five centuries, such as, Arian, Nestorian, and Monophysite churches that made the question unavoidable, how to know whether a particular assembly that calls itself Christian is a true church.

Marks of the Church

The churches allied with the sixteenth-century Reformation in Germany and Switzerland faced the same question. The authenticity of their churches, the Lutheran Church of the Augsburg Confession and the Reformed Protestant Church of Geneva, was called into question by the authorities of the Roman Empire and the Roman Church. Luther wrote in defense of the church of the Reformation, identifying seven marks of the true church: the Word, Baptism, Sacrament of the Altar, the Office of the Keys, the Office of the Ministry, Worship (prayer, public praise, and thanksgiving to God), and the cross (suffering for the sake of the gospel).[15] A church body or a congregation by whatever name is a mixture of true believers and hypocrites, a different distinction than saints and sinners. John Calvin (1509–1564), founder of the Swiss Reformation in Geneva, said the church is a mixed body (*corpus mixtum*). He probably got the idea from Jesus' parable of the wheat and the weeds. The wheat and the weeds grow together. Radical reformers strive to create a pure church, like having a field of wheat without weeds, a church of true believers without hypocrites. In the parable the farm hands asked the owner of the field whether they should get rid of the weeds. He answered, "No, lest in gathering the weeds you root up the wheat along with them. Let both grow together until the harvest."[16] Who are the true believers, the

---

15. Luther, "On the Councils and the Church," 154.
16. Matthew 13:29–30a.

church properly speaking? They are those who are inwardly "born again," with a living faith and a commitment of the heart to Christ and his church. Who are the hypocrites? They are those who belong to the church for reasons of custom, convenience, and outward appearance. It is folly to try to separate the sheep from the goats prematurely, before the harvest. A real hypocrite knows how to disguise his/her hypocrisy.

It may well be that some of the hypocrites hold high ministerial offices in the institutional church—popes, bishops, priests, pastors, teachers, deans, and deacons. Church history does not provide a list of who's who! Every organized church is equipped with leaders, whatever their titles. The Apostle Paul provided a list of leaders in the charismatic churches he served. "God has appointed in the church first apostles, second prophets, third teachers, then workers of miracles, then healers, helpers, administrators, speakers in various kinds of tongues."[17] A generation later many of these special charisms were absorbed into the rudimentary forms of the traditional threefold office of ministry—bishops, elders or presbyters, and deacons.[18] All these forms of ministry have the single purpose of transmitting the fullness of the gospel of Jesus Christ to the succeeding generations of Christians. Christ is the central content of the many ministries in primitive Christianity. The authority in the church is anchored in the authority of Christ; any authority that might arise in the church to usurp his authority is called the antichrist. The first leaders in the church were the apostles, witnesses of the resurrected Jesus. They received their authority directly from Christ and were endowed with Christ's own authority. He said, "He who receives you receives me."[19] "He who hears you hears me."[20] Even today the church's criterion of truth is "what is apostolic." The apostles were evangelists and missionaries and founders of new assemblies called Christian. A church is apostolic if it does what the apostles did—going into the world to preach the gospel and baptize in Jesus' name where the church has not yet been planted.

The question the early church had to face was what to do when all the apostles died. Their legacy was preserved in their writings, which were

17. 1 Corinthians 12:28–30.
18. 1 Timothy 3:1–2, 8; 5:17.
19. Matthew 10:40.
20. Luke 10:16.

circulated and read in their congregations, and in time they became the canon of the New Testament. Some churches believe that that is enough to keep the church apostolic in post-apostolic times. They tout the slogan "Word alone" or in Latin "*sola scriptura.*" Taken at face value this means that the only reliable apostolic succession in the church is what is written in the sixty-six books of the Bible. But this is not what actually happened in the early church. After the apostles died their disciples took over the reins of leadership. In addition to the canon of Scripture the early church equipped itself with the office of ministry. The office-holders were given the title of bishop. This office became an essential ministry to continue apostolic authority in the church. Thus, both canon and office became equally instrumental in keeping the memories and traditions of the apostles alive in the ongoing life of the church. Those appointed to the office of ministry were placed in their position of leadership through prayer and the laying on of hands. Whenever a church has neglected the canonical Scriptures and the office of ministry, she is in danger of becoming an apostate church rather than being an apostolic church.

The Offices of Ministry

In the New Testament a bishop was essentially a pastor of a local congregation. As the church expanded a bishop would have responsibility for multiple congregations in a region or district. Eventually one bishop was elected to oversee the mission of the church at the universal level, a gradual development which accounts for the emergence of the papal office. The conflict between the sixteenth-century Reformers and the Roman Catholic Church did not necessarily result in a Protestant abandonment of the threefold ministerial office of bishops, priests, and deacons, but the tragic schism did limit the jurisdiction of the papal office to those in communion with the Church of Rome. Anglican and most Lutheran Churches have retained the threefold office of bishop, priests/pastors, and deacons. The ecumenical question is whether non-Roman churches continue to hold insuperable objections to the papal office. The official dialogues since the Second Vatican Council between Roman Catholics and other churches—Eastern Orthodox, Anglican, Lutheran, Methodist, and others—have reopened the question of the papal office as a ministry to express the unity of the universal church for the sake its mission to the world.

No New Testament scholars today seriously maintain that Jesus designated Peter as the first pope of Rome. At the same time there is undisputed consensus that Peter held a preeminent place of honor and authority among the twelve disciples. He is the rock on which the church is to be founded; he is entrusted with the keys of the kingdom.[21] Jesus chose Peter to strengthen his brethren in the faith and to feed his sheep.[22] But Peter's failures are also enumerated. All four Gospels report that Peter denied Jesus; he showed lack of faith when he tried to walk on water, and he was rebuked by Jesus saying, "Get behind me, Satan."[23]

Why the later church looked back to Peter and anachronistically dubbed him the first pope is not a church-dividing issue. The dogma of papal infallibility promulgated at the First Vatican Council of 1870 in the document *Pastor Aeternus* continues to be unacceptable to all non-Roman churches. Prescinding from the issue of papal infallibility, non-Roman churches welcome the progress made by the modern ecumenical dialogues in removing many of the traditional objections to the papal office. Just as a pastor ministers to a local congregation, and as a bishop ministers to a wider territory, so the pope's ministry is to the universal communion of churches. A renewed papal ministry must be in the service of the gospel, the global mission of the church, and the purity of biblical-catholic doctrine, and it must be so exercised as not to restrict Christian freedom. Many Roman Catholics today would welcome such a renewal as much as non-Roman Christians.

All churches have had to rethink the authority invested in the offices of ministry, especially in freedom-loving democratic societies opposed to heteronomous structures, infallible officials, and inerrant documents. Who are the ministers of a given church and by what authority do they exercise their office? This question became acute at the time of the Reformation when Roman bishops refused to ordain ministers to serve parishes in Lutheran territories. In response to this crisis Luther suggested that if a group of lay folks were marooned on a desert island, they could choose one amongst them to serve as their pastor, to preach the Word and administer the Sacraments. Such a person would become a pastor without benefit of ordination.

---

21. Matthew 16:18-19.
22. Luke 22:32 and John 21:17.
23. Matthew 14:29-30.

Should an emergency situation become the new normal, whereby the rite (sacrament) of ordination is discontinued and even debunked as a "Romish superstition"? Lutheranism in particular has been bedeviled by the question whether the minister's office is derived from below, that is, from the "priesthood of all believers." The authority of the minister's office is then delegated from the many to the one; this is called the "transference theory." The functions that belong to all the people are transferred to one person, for the sake of order and convenience. This is the low-church view of the ordained ministry.

Opposed to the transference theory is the traditional view that the office of ministry was divinely authorized, called the "institutional theory." In this view God instituted the holy ministry of preaching the gospel and administering the sacraments. A person is authorized to be a minister by ordination, not simply by a majority vote. Ordination is the sign that this office has been divinely instituted (*ius divinum*), and is not based on a human agreement (*ius humanum*). Article 14 of the *Augsburg Confession* stresses, "We say that no one should be allowed to administer the word and sacraments in the church unless he is duly called." "Duly called" translates the Latin "*rite vocatus*," which means ordination. What is ordination? Philip Melanchthon, author of the *Augsburg Confession*, wrote this: "If ordination is interpreted in relation to the ministry of the Word, we have no objection to call ordination a sacrament. . . . If ordination is interpreted in this way, we shall not object either to calling the laying on of hands a sacrament."[24] According to the Lutheran confession, ordination is not merely an installation into an office, like that of a secular magistrate. It is not an adiaphorism, a take-it-or-leave-it proposition, because it ultimately derives from Christ and bestows a spiritual authority to do what is essential to make and keep the church Christian.

After centuries of ambiguity on the doctrine of the ministry the World Council of Churches in 1982 sent 100 delegates, including Roman Catholic representatives, to Lima, Peru, to compose a statement entitled *Baptism, Eucharist and Ministry*. The statement goes far to construct a working consensus that enables churches to acknowledge the validity of each others' ministerial offices. The statement affirms that the ordained ministry is constitutive for the life and witness of the church, even though the New

---

24. Melanchthon, "Apology of the Augsburg Confession," 212.

Testament does not require a particular pattern of ministry. Ministers may be called ambassadors, teachers, pastors, bishops, presbyters, all who are called and ordained to represent Jesus Christ to the people, and not primarily to give voice to the will and wishes of the people. The threefold office of ministry needs to be reformed so that it functions not only as an intramural service to those already Christian, but also that it may recover its New Testament potential to evangelize the nations and revitalize its missional service to the world.

Questions for Discussion

1. The idea of the kingdom of God was central in the message of Jesus, but actually the founding of the church was the result of his ministry. What is the relation between the kingdom of God and the church?

2. There are many images of the church in the New Testament. Which of them do you prefer and why?

3. How does the church of which you are a member relate to the "one, holy, catholic, and apostolic church"?

4. The four attributes of the church, if taken literally, contradict the empirical reality of all the churches on earth. For example, there are many churches, not one, and none are holy. Explain what each of the attributes means in this apparent contradictory situation.

5. Martin Luther identified seven marks of the church. Can you think of any you would like to add to the list, now 500 years later?

6. Some people say they don't belong to the church because it is full of hypocrites. How would you respond?

7. Some churches have bishops, some do not. Some are equipped with the threefold office of ministry, some are not. Does it matter? Why or why not?

10. The Word and Sacraments

The Holy Spirit communicates to individuals the grace of salvation accomplished by the life, death, and resurrection of the incarnate Word, Jesus Christ, by external means—the audible preaching of the Word and the visible administration of the sacraments. Every person who appropriates the proffered gift of salvation by faith is a member of the Christian community, the body of Christ. The church is called and its ministers are ordained to preach a life-giving living Word. The Word the Holy Spirit conveys is the real personal presence of Christ himself, whether the audible Word of the gospel or the visible Word of the sacrament. Martin Luther stressed the importance of the external word in "The Smalcald Articles," 1537. "In these matters, which concern the external, spoken Word, we must hold firmly to the conviction that God gives no one his Spirit or grace except through or with the external Word which comes before.... Accordingly, we should and must constantly maintain that God will not deal with us except through his external Word and sacrament. Whatever is attributed to the Spirit apart from such external Word and sacrament is of the devil."[1] Luther wrote these strong words in opposition to Thomas Müntzer and his followers, whom he called "enthusiasts," because they claimed to have immediate access to the Spirit apart from the external Word of preaching.

The External Word

The external Word in the living voice (*viva vox*) of oral proclamation cannot be separated from the written Word of God. The Holy Spirit does not work in a vacuum; through the words of the Holy Scriptures the revelation of God in Christ is made known to those who have ears to hear. Not only the lively witness to the Word but also the responsive hearing of the Word in a person's heart is the work of the Holy Spirit. In his "Large Catechism,"

---

1. Luther, "The Smalcald Articles," 312, 313.

Luther said this about the Holy Spirit: "Neither you nor I could ever know anything of Christ, or believe in him and take him as our Lord, unless these were first offered to us and bestowed on our hearts through the preaching of the gospel by the Holy Spirit."[2]

Preaching is a means of grace and a mark of the true church. Since it is that important, the church, every church, must take great care to keep it pure, true, and effective. Preaching was the hallmark of the Reformation, preaching the whole counsel of God, both the law and the gospel. Of course, preaching was not the invention of Luther and the Reformation. There were many great preachers in earlier church history, most notably Augustine, Chrysostom, Bernard of Clairvaux, St. Francis, and John Hus. But something new happened with the Reformation. The sermon became the centerpiece of the regular weekly worship service. Before the Reformation preaching happened mostly on special occasions, or for special seasons of the liturgical calendar, such as Christmas and Easter. Because the Reformers gave the sermon the honored place in public worship, the pulpit was raised to a position of prominence and at a higher level, seemingly halfway between heaven and earth. The preacher's lofty and rather distant position led to a certain aloofness from the people. Luther warned against the danger of preachers succumbing to the temptation of prosperity, popularity, and pomposity.

Preachers of the Word are called to be preoccupied with words, day in and day out, morning, noon, and night. They spend a lot of time talking in front of large and small audiences. They are intercessors, **praying to** God for the people and the world. Preachers must also be theologians, that is, know what they are talking about. They are **talking about** God. That is theology, *theos-logos*. This is not possible without a lot of study of Scripture, history, doctrine, language, and culture. Preachers are also ambassadors, not spouting their own opinions, but **speaking for** God as his representatives.

The Law and Gospel of God

The Word of God comes to hearers in two distinct forms with different effects, the law and the gospel. The law of God commands and prohibits; thou shalt do this; thou shalt not do that. Humans are creatures who owe

2. Luther, "The Large Catechism," 415.

10. THE WORD AND SACRAMENTS

their very existence to God and are thus obligated to obey what he says, as children to their parents. The most difficult task for preachers is to draw the proper distinction between the law and the gospel. The main danger is to legalize the gospel, presenting it as something we are supposed to do. The other is to teach the moral law and commandments of God as something we are required to do to please God. Because of sin human beings are incapable of obeying the law of God perfectly. The law accuses the person of failure, drives to repentance, and shows the need for the gospel of forgiveness in Christ. Preaching the law precedes the announcement of the gospel, as the question precedes the answer. Only the gospel can answer the law's demand for perfect obedience and righteousness. The gospel is the story of Christ's vicarious death and victorious resurrection. "Jesus our Lord was put to death for our trespasses and raised for our justification."[3]

It is customary to think of the Old Testament as the book of the law, associated with Moses, the lawgiver, and the New Testament as the book of the gospel, associated with Christ, the Savior. However, the Old Testament is a book that also declares the grace of God and his promise of salvation and the New Testament is also a book of commands and prohibitions. It is possible to preach the gospel from Old Testament texts and to preach the law from New Testament texts. No one preached the severity of God's law more uncompromisingly than Jesus.

The people of God need to be instructed in all purposes of the law that impinges on all dimensions of life. The first purpose of the law is *political*. When preachers are advised not to preach politics, they must not ignore the politics of God's justice and judgment against evil and corruption. The political use of the law rewards those who keep the law and metes out penalties to those who don't. The second purpose of the law is *accusatory*, serving as a mirror of wrongdoing. The law puts the spotlight on a person's shortcomings, ascribes guilt, and drives to despair, the sickness unto death. The third purpose of the law is *pedagogical*, pointing to the need of a solution, indeed, perhaps a Savior. "The law was our schoolmaster to bring us unto Christ."[4] The law in itself does not know or teach anything about Christ, but indirectly it can bestir a person to seek what Christ has to offer. The fourth purpose of the law is *didactic*, teaching people the

3. Romans 4:25.
4. Galatians 3:24.

basic rules of life, the difference between right and wrong, the natural law that is written on human hearts from birth, and for Jews and Christians, the Ten Commandments.

The gospel is specifically what God has accomplished for salvation in the life, death, and resurrection of Jesus Christ. Salvation in Christ means forgiveness of sins, righteousness before God, and eternal life, received by faith with a thankful heart, apart from the need to perform meritorious works prescribed by the law. Here we are broaching the subject of justification, which for Luther and his reforming colleagues was the "article by which the church stands and falls."[5] We will resume the discussion of the doctrine of justification in the next chapter on "The Church and the World."

The Sacraments

There is no agreement among the Christian churches on the sacraments, not even on what is a sacrament. The term itself is not in the Bible and its origin is from outside the church. Sacrament comes from a Latin term for a military oath of allegiance that was taken over by the church to refer to something sacred. The Greek term for sacrament is *mysterion* and is still used in Eastern Orthodoxy. Its Latin translation is sacrament, used by all churches in Western Christianity, even though they do not agree on its meaning, usage, or how many there are.

St. Augustine defined a sacrament as "an outward and visible sign of an inward and invisible grace." Most churches can agree with this definition, but it does not answer the question of how many rites or ceremonies of the church are sacraments. At the Council of Trent (1545–1563) the Roman Catholic Church decided on seven sacraments. Protestants have waffled between two and three sacraments. In addition to Baptism and the Lord's Supper, the Lutheran "Apology of the Augsburg Confession," written by Philip Melanchthon, calls absolution—the office of the keys—a sacrament of penitence because it offers the gospel of forgiveness. There is no question that all Christians need the forgiveness of sins. The sacrament of penitence is an ancient rite of the church to deal with the sins of its members, even though there is no record of a dominical institution of such a rite in the New Testament. Since the Reformation the practice of absolution has been

---

5. The *Articulus stantis et cadentis ecclesiae*.

continued in Protestant Churches, although irregularly and inconsistently. Even in Roman Catholicism private confession and absolution have declined at the parish level. Protestant Churches that still practice general confession and absolution in their weekly communion service generally do not think of that ceremony as a sacrament. Moreover, the traditional practice of private confession and absolution has been transformed into what is called "pastoral counseling." Baptism and the Lord's Supper are universally regarded as sacraments because they were clearly instituted by Christ and are constituted by two essential things, the Word and a material element. In baptism the material element or sign is water and in the Lord's Supper bread and wine are the physical signs.

The modern ecumenical movement has challenged churches to give renewed attention to sacramental theology, in view of the fact that the Roman Catholic Church continues to treat seven ritual ceremonies as sacraments. For what reason have Protestants in general retained only two sacraments, baptism and the Lord's Supper? Even this question needs further qualification. Mainline Protestant Churches that are members of the World Council of Churches have generally responded positively to the Faith and Order Statement of 1982, *Baptism, Eucharist and Ministry*, which represents a remarkable theological convergence on two sacraments. This statement, called the Lima Text, was agreed to by 100 theologians that represented major church traditions, including Eastern Orthodox, Roman Catholic, and Mainline Protestant. However, large segments of modern Protestantism are non-sacramental churches and do not participate in the ecumenical movement. Baptists, Churches of Christ, Mennonites, Pentecostal, and others regard Baptism and the Lord's Supper as ordinances to be observed because Jesus instituted them, but merely as professions of faith and not as means of God's grace.

The seven church ceremonies defined as sacraments by the Roman Catholic Church are: Baptism, Confirmation, Penance, Eucharist, Anointing the Sick, Ordination, and Marriage. At the time that Philip Melanchthon wrote his book of doctrine, *Loci Communes,* in 1543, the treatment of the sacraments was rather fluid. There is no hard and fast rule in Scripture or the church's theology of the first five centuries to limit the sacraments to any particular number. The inter-confessional dialogues between Catholics and other churches has had the beneficial effect of reopening the question of the nature and number of the sacraments. Melanchthon was open to listing ordination among the sacraments. He wrote, "In my opinion there is considerable merit in adding also ordination [as a sacrament], that is, the call into the ministry of the Gospel and the public approval of this call, because all these things are enjoined as injunctions of the Gospel."[6] On the other hand, Melanchthon was not so sanguine about regarding confirmation as a sacrament. He affirmed its usefulness as a ritual examination of confirmands instructed in the doctrines of the faith, accompanied by public prayer and the laying on of hands, bestowing on them gifts of the Holy Spirit. He lamented that in his time the rite had become an exclusive prerogative of bishops, rendering it, as he said, "an absolutely useless ceremony."[7] Whether sacrament or not, the practice of confirmation in most churches has become sporadic for lack of a coherent theological justification.

The sacrament of anointing the sick with oil has its precedent in the healing miracles of Jesus and in the apostolic church. It is written in James 5:14–15: "Is any among you sick? Let him call for the elders of the church, and let them pray over him, anointing him with oil in the name of the Lord; and the prayer of faith will save the sick man, and the Lord will raise him up; and if he has committed sins, he will be forgiven." Melanchthon admits that this gift of healing continued to be practiced subsequently in the church and that many are still healed by the prayers of the church. God wants this to be fostered in the church in the right away. However, this sacrament too has succumbed to malpractice. He said, "The rite of anointing as it now exists is only a superstitious ceremony. And invocation of the dead was added, which is ungodly. Therefore this rite of unction with its additions is to be rejected."[8]

Baptism

Whereas there is considerable divergence on a number of the sacraments, the opposite is true with respect to the sacrament of baptism among ecumenically engaged churches. The "Decree on Ecumenism" of Vatican II and the Faith and Order Lima Text, "Baptism, Eucharist and Ministry," both affirmed that baptism is a bond of unity among Christians of all

6. Melanchthon, *Loci Communes*, 140.
7. Melanchthon, *Loci Communes*, 142.
8. Melanchthon, *Loci Communes*, 142.

persuasions. There is no such thing as being baptized Methodist or Anglican or Catholic or any other denomination. A person is baptized with water in the name of the triune God, and as such becomes a member of the body of Christ, the one, holy, catholic, and apostolic church. Baptism does not erase the doctrinal differences among the various denominations, but it does transcend divisions into a unity created by the Spirit of God the Father and the Son. Even at the time of the Reformation Lutherans and Catholics recognized the validity of each others' baptism, and both also opposed the rebaptizers, the Anabaptists, who refused to baptize infants and regarded baptism as a subjective profession of faith, not as a sacrament objectively offering the gift of divine grace.

What is baptism and what does it do? Baptism is something that Jesus commanded his disciples to do: "Go therefore and make disciples of all nations, baptizing them into the name of the Father and the Son and of the Holy Spirit."[9] Baptism is a sacrament of initiation, the beginning of the person's new life in Christ, and at the same time an open invitation to eat and drink at the table of the Lord. Those who welcome the unbaptized to participate in the Lord's Supper are either guilty of invincible ignorance or willful malpractice. Likewise, churches that forbid baptized believers from holy communion must answer the question why they have turned the Lord's Supper into their Church's Supper. The Christian confession based on the New Testament is that Jesus is Lord of the universal church, of all who believe and are baptized, not only of those who belong to the particular denomination that happens to bear the name of its founder, ethnic group, or place of origin.

Baptism is a rite ordained by God, promising the righteousness of Christ to those who believe. In case of adults baptism is certainly something the recipients do to express their faith; but more importantly it is first and foremost the act of God for salvation in Christ that makes Christians members of his body. And baptism is a once-for-all act. Just as an individual is born once, just so a Christian is born again, only once, never to be repeated. Churches that require a second baptism do not understand the meaning and efficacy of baptism. Traditionally the mode of baptism is optional, either by immersion or pouring. A handful of water is sufficient, but a mere drop or two loses the visual power of the act. A few churches

---

9. Matthew 28:19.

restrict baptism to adults by immersion only; for them baptism is an act of dedication with symbolic meaning, not a sacrament of regeneration and sanctification empowered by the Holy Spirit. "But when the goodness and lovingkindness of God our Savior appeared, he saved us, not because of deeds done by us in righteousness, but in virtue of his own mercy, by the washing of regeneration and renewal in the Holy Spirit, which he poured out upon us richly through Jesus Christ our Savior."[10]

The saving effect of baptism continues throughout the life of Christians, in good times and bad. Luther wrote:

> In Baptism, therefore, every Christian has enough to study and to practice all his life. He always has enough to do to believe firmly what Baptism promises and brings—victory over death and the devil, forgiveness of sin, God's grace, the entire Christ, and the Holy Spirit with his gifts.... To appreciate and use Baptism aright, we must draw strength and comfort from it when our sins or conscience oppress us, and we must retort, "But I am baptized! And if I am baptized, I have the promise that I shall be saved and have eternal life, both soul and body."[11]

Here we are assured that baptism is the alpha and omega of the Christian life, reaching from the beginning of life here and now to the eschatological end, with the glorious promise of resurrection from death and everlasting life. For this reason every day can be a return to baptism by which the mind is enlightened by the gifts of the Holy Spirit and the will is liberated to obey the laws of God in deeds of love and justice. Here the return to baptism and the sacrament of penitence substantially converge.

The validity of infant baptism has become a problem that families are inevitably forced to face due to an increase of mixed marriages. Scholarly monographs have been written on baptism in the apostolic age with no clear resolution on whether infants of Christian parents were baptized at that time. It is certain that in the course of history the baptism of infants became common practice, but always with the proviso that baptized infants will receive Christian nurture so that later they can make their own personal confession of faith. The rite of confirmation has been the church's way of ensuring that the full promise of baptism will be realized in the recipient's

---

10. Titus 3:4–6.
11. Luther, "Large Catechism," 442.

faithful participation in the life of the church. Either by divine inspiration or common sense pastors are loathe to baptize minors of non-Christian parents, since they cannot promise to raise their children in "the knowledge and the fear of the Lord."[12]

The Lord's Supper

The Sacrament of the Altar is known by different names in church history—the Lord's Supper, Holy Communion, Eucharist. Sometimes it is simply referred to as the Supper or the Meal. The practices also vary from church to church. The modern liturgical movement in tandem with the ecumenical movement created a new situation in which churches have been learning from each other, adopting different ways to celebrate the sacrament and new language to conceptualize its meaning. Some churches believe that what makes the sacrament is the recitation of the very words Jesus' used at the Last Supper in the Upper Room on Maundy Thursday. Some churches do not believe that a properly called and ordained minister is necessary to preside at the service. They are likely to see that as sacerdotalism, or even derisively as priestly hocus-pocus.

Churches that stem from the magisterial Reformation of Martin Luther are generally unfamiliar with much of the terminology expressed in the liturgical reforms. Some oppose making any changes to accommodate new practices, fearing deviation from orthodoxy. Others are open to learn new practices so long as they do not displace what they believe to be essential. Based on biblical and patristic studies, the liturgical movement rediscovered forgotten treasures in liturgical worship and sacramental practices. Changes were not proposed for the sake of change nor for the sake of novelty, but to retrieve ancient patterns of observance forgotten or replaced. Many denominations do not call the Lord's Supper the Eucharist. Their liturgy does not include the "Great Thanksgiving," and they prefer to talk about the sacrifice of praise rather than speaking of the Eucharist as sacrifice, lest that detracts from Christ's unique unrepeatable sacrifice on the cross. The concept of *anamnesis* that refers to the sacrifice as a memorial reminds Lutherans of the Marburg Colloquy where Luther and Zwingli diverged on the real presence of Christ's body and blood in the elements of bread and wine. For Lutherans the body and blood of Christ are really

12. Isaiah 11:2.

present "in, with, and under" the signs of bread and wine, and these are not merely symbolic reminders of his sacrificial death on the cross. The *Epiclesis,* a prayer invoking the presence of the Holy Spirit, is virtually absent in the Reformation tradition. But may it not be acceptable to conceive of the Holy Spirit as present and active in the words of Jesus, "This is my body. . . . This is my blood," to make Christ really present? The works of the Spirit and the Word are always closely linked in the New Testament.

The Lima Text *Baptism, Eucharist, and Ministry* is an ecumenical invitation to all participating churches to consider whether they may not beneficially learn from each other, revitalize their own liturgical practices, engage in the process of reconciling their historic differences, and strive for a common witness across denominational borders.

The simpler celebrations of the Lord's Supper administered in the Reformation tradition are being enriched by the wealth of new practices that other communions contribute to liturgical renewal, as new books of worship periodically replace older ones. The areas of challenge that invite serious reflection have to do with naming the Lord's Supper the Eucharist, and with a range of related concepts such as the "Great Thanksgiving," "*Anamnesis*" or "Memorial," "*Epiclesis*" or "Invocation of the Spirit," "Sacrifice" as representation, and reserving the elements.

Before innovations are welcomed in the name of liturgical renewal, it is important to have a clear compendium of teaching that articulates what is essential and what may be *adiaphora* in the celebration of the Lord's Supper. There is always a threat that so many mysterious things are happening at once—words, rubrics, gestures, bells, smoke, vestments—that the central content of the celebration becomes obscured—the real presence of Christ as the host of the meal bestowing the full forgiveness of sins to repentant sinners and the promise of eternal life. Diversity within limits is not the problem, but deviation from the core features of the Lord's Supper according to the New Testament is.

The following section intends to convey the basic features of a scriptural understanding of the Lord's Supper. Observance of the Lord's Supper consists of four perceptible components: Christ's words of institution, bread and wine, a community of believers, and a presiding minister of the church. What this means for the participants is imperceptible, without which the observance would not be worth the effort. Only the eyes of faith sees this event as the real presence of Christ in his body and blood. Without the spoken Word the bread and wine would be merely ordinary bread and wine and not the body and blood of Christ. The Word is communicated through the words Christ used when he instituted the Supper in the presence of his disciples. If these words are omitted, the performance of the sacrament is a nullity. After the administration of the sacrament is concluded, the bread and wine remain bread and wine. There is no basis in Scripture to believe otherwise.

Jesus intended that his institution of the Supper would be the first of others to follow. He said, "Do this in remembrance of me." He told them what they are to do; he commanded them to eat and drink. "Take, eat; this is my body. . . . Drink of it, all of you; for this is my blood."[13] What they are to eat is not merely bread; what they are to drink is not merely wine. It is the body and blood of Christ, that is, "the whole Christ." [14] What is happening is really physical, not merely spiritual. But what for? The forgiveness of sins that was accomplished on the cross of Christ is now being given to each recipient. This means that the community's eating and drinking here and now does not only repeat, symbolize, and memorialize what happened once upon a time, which would make it merely subjective. The words "shed for you" and "given to you" indicate that something objective is happening, making every celebration a contemporaneous event in which the whole Christ is really and personally present in his divine and human natures. The whole Christ is the exalted Christ, personally identical with the crucified and risen body of Christ. Christ is present bodily, and therefore he is present wherever and whenever the sacrament is celebrated according to the words of institution. Zwingli's idea that Christ cannot be bodily present because he is locally situated at the right hand of God in heaven introduces metaphysics into the doctrine of the Lord's Supper, with no scriptural justification. The institution of the Lord's Supper is reported in all three Synoptic Gospels, Matthew, Mark, and Luke, and in Paul's First Letter to the Corinthians. None of them speculate on how in every celebration of the sacrament it is possible for Christ to be really present in his body and blood with the bread and wine. Subsequently various theories have been

13. Matthew 26:26–28.
14. Matthew 26:28.

conceived to explain how Christ can be so present, from transubstantiation, consubstantiation, impanation, or whatever. Luther himself speculated with his idea of ubiquity, but no speculative theory is needed to validate the sacrament. Dogmatics has no interest in deciding among the various theories, because the essential truth is not at stake.

The Apostle Paul warns the Corinthians that "whoever eats the bread or drinks the cup of the Lord in an unworthy manner will be guilty of profaning the body and blood of the Lord. Let a man examine himself, and so eat of the bread and drink of the cup. For anyone who eats and drinks without discerning the body eats and drinks judgment upon himself."[15] This warning urges all members of the Christian community to be prepared to eat and drink with Jesus as guests at his table, lest they show up with a contemptuous and thoughtless attitude. Eating and drinking worthily means to believe what the words of institution say, ready to accept the gift of forgiveness of sins, life, and salvation by faith. Faith is not a feeling of one's worthiness; faith is radical receptivity of the gift with an open hand, an open mind, an open heart. For unbelievers to be welcomed to the Supper is sacrilege, an invitation to eat and drink in an unworthy manner, exposing them to spiritual harm and judgment. There is no scriptural basis for the opinion that unbelievers receive only the bread and the wine, so there's nothing to worry about. The truth is that by not discerning the body, there's nothing good or profitable that can come of it. It is pastorally more prudent to reserve the celebration of the sacrament to those for whom Jesus instituted it, for his faithful followers, and only for them.

Questions for Discussion

1. What is the ecclesial significance of what Martin Luther meant by the "external word" (*verbum externum*)?
2. An ordained minister of the church is called to do a lot of speaking in behalf of the congregation. What are the various modes of such oral communication?
3. What is the function of the law? Theologians have argued about whether there are two or three uses of the law. What is the controversy all about?

---

15. 1 Corinthians 11:27–29.

10. THE WORD AND SACRAMENTS

4. Can you state what the gospel is in one sentence? Is there one verse in the Bible that does so?
5. What is at stake in the controversy over the number of sacraments, two or three or seven?
6. Some churches are against infant baptism. Some churches do not believe baptism is a sacrament. What is baptism? How should it be administered in a post-Christendom age?
7. Discuss the Lord's Supper controversy between Luther and Zwingli. What is the meaning of "real presence," and how does it relate to the idea of the Lord's Supper as a "memorial" or "commemoration"?

11. The Church and the World

What God has done in Jesus Christ for the salvation of the world laid the foundation for what Christians are to do in the world. Christianity is an eschatological religion; it began with Jesus' proclamation of the eschatological kingdom of God, which already arrived in his life, death, and resurrection according to the apostolic witness, but the world continued thereafter to exist pretty much as usual, indicating that the kingdom in its fullness had not yet come. Eschatology deals with the future and final apocalyptic end of all things that God has in store for the world. Ethics is the discipline that deals with the church's responsibility for the concrete world in all its complex dimensions. This chapter focuses on what the Christian people of the endtime are to do in the meantime. Christians live between the times, between the new age (*aeon*) which has already dawned in the coming of Jesus Christ and overlaps the old age which continues under the providence of God and has not yet come to a close.

The Doctrine of Justification

The Apostle Paul is the clearest New Testament teacher of the gospel of God's grace and justification of sinners through faith apart from the works of the law. As a Pharisee he knew the teaching of the Hebrew Scriptures that the justice of God calls for righteousness measured by obedience to his law. By the same teaching he knew that human beings are slaves of sin and guilty before God. Then Paul had his Damascus Road experience of encountering the risen Christ and his whole theology was turned upside down. The righteousness demanded by the law in order to enjoy true fellowship with God is not possible for sinners. Then he heard and learned the gospel of God: the righteousness of Christ is communicated by God's grace and received by faith alone,[1] not on the basis of law and works of

---

1. See Jenson, *Lutheran Slogans, Use and Abuse*.

merit. The condition of being right with God is a free gift of grace, never the result of human accomplishment. This teaching became the heart of Luther's interpretation of the gospel. Justification of sinners by God's grace alone through faith alone on account of Christ alone is the article by which the church stands and falls.

The doctrine of justification has been at the forefront of the intensive modern ecumenical dialogues between Lutherans and Catholics, culminating in the "Joint Declaration on the Doctrine of Justification." While the two communions have had different ways of talking about justification, their common statement is sufficient to assure both sides that their linguistic differences are no longer church-dividing. They agree that all persons depend completely on the saving grace of God for their salvation, that God forgives sin by grace and at the same time frees human beings from sin's enslaving power and imparts the gift of new life in Christ, that sinners are justified by faith in the saving action of God in Christ, that persons are justified by faith in the gospel apart from works prescribed by the law, that good works follow justification and are its fruits. The only thing these assertions lack are the three Lutheran *solas*—*sola gratia, sola fide, solus Christus*. Paul's teaching about justification does not use the word *sola*. Luther used the word to stress that righteousness comes by faith without the works of the law, and that means, Luther said, by faith alone. And when Paul said, "without the works of the law," that is the same as saying, "solely by faith."

"Faith alone" does not mean that faith is ever alone. Faith is active in love doing works that serve the neighbor. The faith that justifies before God wrought by the Holy Spirit regenerates and sanctifies the sinner. Faith is not an idle thing; it is busy, active, lively, potent, creative, imaginative, seeking ways to do good, to perform works of love, to serve those in need. Faith itself is a good work; it is the work of God the Holy Spirit. Faith is known by its fruits. Faith comes first, good works follow, as a tree brings forth good fruit.

The message of justification by faith seeks expression in the various callings, vocations, professions, occupations, or obligations that Christians live out in the real world. No one vocation is more Christian than another. God may call a Christian to be a minister, or farmer, police officer, butcher, painter, teacher, soldier, or whatever, and all of them are equally sacred and secular. Christians are not sent to work by God to do a boring job; rather they are called to obey God by serving their neighbors in daily life, and there are myriad ways to do that. Justification by faith brings forgiveness of sins, paradoxically giving peace of mind and a joyful spirit, even while doing daily duties, often not without drudgery, humiliation, toil, and turmoil. Christians can take the words of Jesus literally, "Therefore do not be anxious about tomorrow, for tomorrow will be anxious for itself. Let the day's own trouble be sufficient for the day."[2]

First Thessalonians discloses that some of the first generation of Christians believed that the Lord would return in their lifetime and put an end to the world.[3] There have been self-appointed prophets in every succeeding generation who have predicted the exact year of the second coming of Christ. Such eschatological enthusiasm is liable to cut the nerve of Christian involvement in the affairs of this world. But leaders in the early church counseled otherwise. In the second century an anonymous writer wrote a "Letter to Diognetus." The letter survived but it is not known who Diognetus was nor the identity of the author. He wrote that though Christians live "in" the world like everyone else, they are not "of" the world.

> Christians are not distinguished from the rest of humanity by country, language, or custom. For nowhere do they live in cities of their own, nor do they speak some unusual dialect, nor do they practice an eccentric life-style.... But while they live in both Greek and Barbarian cities, as each one's lot was cast, and follow the local customs in dress and food and other aspects of life, at the same time they demonstrate the remarkable and admittedly unusual character of their own citizenship. They live in their own countries, and endure everything as foreigners. Every foreign country is their fatherland, and every fatherland is foreign. They marry like everyone else, and have children, but they do not expose their offspring. They share their food but not their wives. They are "in the flesh," but they do not live "according to the flesh." They live on earth, but their citizenship is in heaven. They obey the established laws; indeed in their private lives they transcend the laws.[4]

St. Augustine is the most important church father who wrote about the church's social and political responsibility. In his magnum opus, *City of God*, he contrasted two cities, the city of God and the city of this world,

---

2. Matthew 6:34.
3. 1 Thessalonians 4:13-17.
4. "Letter to Diognetus," 5: 1-10.

11. THE CHURCH AND THE WORLD

the earthly city. The goal or purpose of each city is to seek a life of peace; the difference is that the city of God promises a life of everlasting peace, whereas the earthly city can at best provide an imperfect peace. True peace and happiness can only be experienced in fellowship with God. In the earthly city there is no lasting peace, not between nations, not in family life, and not within each individual soul. Yet, for Augustine Christians are citizens of both cities, the city of God and the earthly city. As full citizens of the earthly city they bear responsibility for the measure of peace, order, and flourishing it can attain. They may serve as mayors, judges, teachers, even soldiers, engaged in serving and securing the common good along with those who are not Christians. All are subject to the same laws and participate in the same institutions. Power and punishment are inescapably necessary to deal with the prevalence of sin and evil in the fallen world, for Christians and non-Christians alike.

Martin Luther was an Augustinian monk and a student of Augustine's theology. Like Augustine he had a robust view of the Christian's responsibility for life in the earthly city. He did not believe that only Christians possessed knowledge and understanding of the realities of government and law. God established them prior to the incarnation of Jesus Christ and the founding of the community in his name. The social and political activity of the God of the Bible is universal, beyond the limits of his special revelation in Jesus Christ. God reveals his power and will through the structures of creation and the natural law knowable by reason and conscience. This means that there is no need for a specifically "Christian" politics or "Christian" legislation. God has two ways of working in the world, through the state (government) and the law and through the church and the gospel, and they have different aims and purposes. This has been called the doctrine of the two kingdoms, often misunderstood and misapplied when the two kingdoms are so separated as to have nothing to do with each other. When this happens, Christians in politics and business feel justified in leaving their conscience at the door when they enter their place of work.

As a professor of the Old Testament Luther knew very well that the living God was at work among the peoples of the world prior to and apart from his covenant with his chosen people of Israel. For example, the Lord God of Israel chose Cyrus, king of Persia, to liberate his people from their Babylonian captivity and return to Jerusalem. God rules in the world and is active through the law whether anyone knows it or not. Kings and dictators are subject to the law and purposes of God whether they know it or not. There is no sphere of life from which God is absent. God acts in all realms of life through the demands he makes on individuals, pressuring them behind their backs to do what their conscience compels them to do. The Second Table of the Law has to do with honoring parents, with prohibiting murder, sexual deviancy, stealing, lying, coveting, matters applicable in all societies. No word of special revelation is necessary to make them known. In Luther's apt terminology, this is the work of the left hand of God. The gospel of Jesus Christ, the central event in the biblical history of salvation from alpha to omega, is the work of the right hand of God.

Jesus commissioned his disciples to go to all the nations with the gospel, to teach and to baptize in the name of the Father and of the Son and of the Holy Spirit. At the same time the church must also manifest concern for this world, solving problems, seeking peace and justice, and caring especially for those in greatest need. It is wrong for Christians to withdraw from worldly responsibility into spiritual enclaves of only their own kind. The church penetrates the world not only through its individual members, who meet their responsibilities in their sundry callings. The church is also a corporate reality, with responsibility to act as a body within the social sphere.

The church is called to behave in the world according to its God-given assignment to be light, salt, and leaven. True worship of God results in an obedient life of service. The gospel is the solution to the ultimate problem of how sinners stand before God. The law functions in the sphere of the penultimate, seeking practical solutions in the domain of public life. The church as a reconciled community in Christ can be a leaven that permeates the whole society, affecting the ideal of justice and the administration of law. When blacks and whites marched together under the leadership of Martin Luther King, they bore witness to their common humanity created in the image of God. But when they knelt together at the table of the Lord, eating from the one loaf and drinking from the one cup, they were reconciled in the one body of Christ. As reconciled brothers and sisters they were dismissed to serve the Lord by changing social structures that institutionalized racial estrangement and segregation, at the beach, in restaurants, public transportation, labor unions, and social fraternities. The church's worship of God does not offer a blueprint for a better society,

11. THE CHURCH AND THE WORLD

but it does leave an indelible imprint on the redeemed conscience of its faithful members.

Why should Christians and churches take the lead in the struggle for human rights, for the rights of children, the not yet born, minorities, women, heretics, imprisoned, or those who suffer from any kind of social, religious, political, racial, or ethnic discrimination? There is one good reason—the example of Jesus, Lord and Savior. He showed it in his way with children, sinners, lepers, thieves, women, prostitutes, outcasts, the poor and the rich. He loved them, accepted them, healed them, fed them, and restored their dignity. Jesus did not mince words. He said, "Woe to you that are rich!" The huge discrepancy between the rich and the poor is unacceptable by the standards of Jesus' kingdom ethics. He warned that it is virtually impossible for rich people to inherit the kingdom of God. One wealthy person was told to sell everything he owned and give to the poor. St. Francis of Assisi took Jesus' words literally, and many mendicant friars followed suit. Most of Jesus' followers have dealt with Jesus' hard saying by taking them figuratively. Once the church became an established institution in Christendom, court theologians depoliticized the message of Jesus to make the church's hierarchs political eunuchs for the kingdom's sake. Jesus was not a social reformer, nor a political revolutionary, like one of the zealots. He was not a politician. He was unique; no worldly category is fitting to describe his way of being and acting. But Jesus did die as a political criminal for subverting the things that Caesar wanted to make Rome the supreme power on earth. Jesus was a threat to the religious establishment of Jerusalem and the political establishment of Rome. Not long after Jesus was crucified, the early Christians declared his death on the cross the event of salvation for Jews and Gentiles, and for the whole world.

Christians have responsibility for other spheres of secular life in addition to the social and political, such as the economy, sexuality (marriage and family), agriculture (food and farming), and ecology (care for the planet). The love of God for Christ's sake inspires Christians to join the struggle for freedom from poverty, hunger, misery, oppression, and ignorance. God is at work through Christians and people of other faiths or no faith at all to join in the work to make things right between human beings, genders, races, and nations and to resist those guilty of violating the rights of others simply because they have the power, position, privilege and the wherewithal to do that.

The church is equipped with the necessary resources to exhibit its love for God and all neighbors through works of mercy and justice. First of all, the church is to preach the whole counsel of God, which includes not only the gospel of salvation but also the politics of the kingdom by means of law and justice (the *regnum potentiae* and the *usis legis politicus*). Second, the church intercedes for the victims of oppression whose rights are negated in any way. Third, the church is to model before the world how human beings can live together fully respecting one another's rights. Fourth, the church calls upon all its members to practice the Christian life through their daily vocations. Fifth, the church is to be a watchdog, militantly vigilant against forces at work to deprive people of their basic rights. Sixth, the church is called to take the side of those whose rights are being trampled down by the powers that be. Seventh, the church must teach it members to be socially sensitive to new forms of oppression and to put the spotlight of compassion on its invisible victims.

The Economy

The Christian church has received a special revelation of God concerning the way of salvation in the name of Jesus Christ for all human beings. Jesus commanded his disciples to preach the gospel to all nations, a mission only the church is called to carry out. At the same time the church lives in the world that God created and that continues under his providential care. Through his general revelation God calls all human beings to care for each other and the world he loves. This revelation is given through the law of creation accessible to all human beings through reason, conscience, and common sense. Christians are called not only to do their part, but also to bear witness to the law of God that relates to all structures of creation, including the economic order. The church acting as an organized institution or through its individual members knows that it has received from its sacred Scriptures no blueprint for how to organize society or manage its economic life. Christians may be socialists to the left, capitalists to the right, or halfway between both, all feeling equally free to exercise their responsibility in whatever way they deem is most beneficial for the common good, defined by principles of equality, justice, and peace. While Christians are free to act according to their conscience, that does not mean their choices are all equally right and sound. All too frequently Christians have supported wicked leaders, dictators, war lords, murderers, liars, cheaters, to serve their own self-interests, social position, racial identity, or economic privilege. Millions of Christians and churches in the twentieth century were guilty of supporting Hitler, Stalin, Mussolini, and Mao Tse Tung, all dictators who built and operated mechanisms of mass murder.

Since pastors and theologians have no special expertise on the market economy or on economic matters in general, it is fair to ask: What do Christians and their churches have to bring to the discussions and decisions that concern the economic life of their societies and that also affect the international order? They are heirs of something very valuable—a heritage of social and economic wisdom mediated through the biblical prophets, the moral teachings of Jesus, and the ethical writings of great Christian minds—church fathers like Origen and Augustine, medieval scholastics like St. Thomas and St. Bonaventure, church reformers like Luther and Calvin, and modern social activists like Dorothy Day and Martin Luther King. Their reflections on the meaning of the Seventh Commandment, "You shall not steal," have much to contribute to the formation of the Christian conscience in every generation. A common thread that runs through the entire biblical-Christian tradition is the negative impact of money and material possessions on the economic life of societies. A major concern is the relation between the rich and the poor and the gap between affluent and impoverished nations. A few samples of these concerns will indicate what inquiring Christians may discover when they seek how best to exercise their social responsibility and vote their conscience as believers in Christ and members of his church.

The starting point is given in the first chapter of Genesis, where it states emphatically that God created human beings, male and female, after his image and likeness to be stewards of his whole creation, to have dominion over everything, the fish of the sea, the birds of the air, beasts of the earth, all trees and green plants for food. All these things in God's whole creation belong to all human beings. Thus, when the world's goods are divided up and distributed by laws of private ownership, this must be regulated in such a way as not to favor the strong and not to deny the weak, so destructive of the fundamental solidarity of the whole human race. Christians who own money and property know that as good stewards of what belongs to God, they are not to horde their possessions for their own benefit but to manage everything in the end for the welfare of all. The Golden Rule never loses it pertinence: Do unto others as you would have them do unto you.

Consider Martin Luther's explanation of the seventh commandment: "We should fear and love God, and so we should not rob our neighbor of his money or property, nor bring them into our possession by dishonest trade or by dealing in shoddy wares, but help him to improve and protect his income and property."[5] There are many ways of stealing: defrauding someone in a business deal, not paying a just wage for services rendered, lying about taxes to the state or federal government, not observing all provisions of a contract, selling a damaged product like a used car without full disclosure to the prospective buyer. Zacchaeus, a rich man, said to Jesus, "'Behold, Lord, the half of my goods I give to the poor; and if I have defrauded any one of anything, I restore it fourfold.' And Jesus said to him, 'Today salvation has come to this house.'"[6] St. Paul lived at a time when slavery was allowed. He told a Christian slave owner no longer to treat a slave as a slave but as a brother in Christ.[7]

As stewards of creation, assigned by the Creator to have dominion over the earth, it is not a far stretch for Christians to care for all God's creatures, for the care of animals and pets, for the care of the lakes, rivers, and seas, for the air and the skies, for the integrity of the entire planet earth. There is an economic price to pay when caring for all the earth's resources. However, in every society there are those motivated more by what profits themselves than what promotes the common good. "For the love of money is the root of all evils; it is through this craving that some have wandered away from their faith."[8] Those who are mastered by money can no longer have God as their Lord. "No one can serve two masters; for either he will hate the one and love the other, or he will be devoted to the one and despise the other. You cannot serve God and mammon."[9] The economic life of a nation is a necessity—producing goods and services to provide for the needs of its

---

5. Luther, "The Small Catechism," 343.
6. Luke 19:8.
7. Philemon 16.
8. 1 Timothy 6:10.
9. Matthew 6:24.

citizens. This is done inevitably for profit, or it won't get done at all. For Christians the profit motive to benefit oneself and one's family is important, yet it is kept in tandem with the desire to serve others.

Christians bring a strong work ethic to the economic life of their societies. As stewards of creation, called to replenish and subdue the earth, work is their God-given vocation.[10] "If anyone will not work, let him not eat."[11] Sloth is one of the seven cardinal sins. St. Thomas Aquinas said sloth is "sluggishness of the mind . . . evil in its effects."

Economic justice means that workers deserve to be paid a wage sufficient to provide a decent living for themselves and their families. Workers have a right to strike when business enterprises put profits above their welfare. Luther's explanation of the seventh commandment targets businesses that take advantage of their workers, whether

> in a grocery shop, butcher stall, wine-and-beer cellars, workshop, and, in short, wherever business is transacted and money is exchanged for goods or labor. . . . They openly cheat others with defective merchandise, false measures, dishonest weights, and bad coins, and take advantage of them by underhanded tricks and sharp practices and crafty dealing. . . . They are called gentlemen swindlers or big operators, they sit in office chairs and are called great lords and princes and daily plunder not only a city or two but all Germany. . . . This commandment is very far reaching. . . . Daily the poor are defrauded. New burdens and high prices are imposed. Everyone misuses the market in his own willful, conceited, arrogant way, as if it were his right and privilege to sell his goods as dearly as he pleases without a word of criticism. . . . Beware how you deal with the poor. . . . God, who watches over poor, sorrowful hearts, will not leave them unavenged.[12]

The Christian love for the poor is deeply rooted in the sayings of Jesus.

> "Give to him who begs from you, and do not refuse him who would borrow from you."[13]

---

10. Genesis 1:28.
11. 2 Thessalonians 3:10.
12. Luther, "Large Catechism," 395–98.
13. Matthew 5:42.

> "For I was hungry and you gave me food, I was thirsty and you gave me drink, I was a stranger and you welcomed me, I was naked and you clothed me, I was sick and you visited me, I was in prison and you visited me. . . . Truly, I say to you, as you did it to one of the least of these my brethren, you did it to me."[14]

Passages such as these made such an impression on St. Francis of Assisi (1182–1226) that he gave up a life of luxury due to his father's wealth for a life devoted to poverty, and eventually founded the Franciscan Order of Friars. With some imagination Christians will try to translate their responsibility for the poor to advocacy of international monetary policies that encourage rich nations to come to the aid of poor nations. What they read in James 5:1–5 will haunt them if they do not try.

> Come now, you rich, weep and howl for the miseries that are coming upon you. Your riches have rotted and your garments are moth-eaten. Your gold and silver have rusted, and their rust will be evidence against you and will eat your flesh like fire. You have laid up treasure for the last days. Behold the wages of the laborers who mowed your fields, which you kept back by fraud, cry out, and the cries of the harvesters have reached the ears of the Lord of hosts. You have lived on the earth in luxury and in pleasure; you have fattened your hearts in a day of slaughter.

Sex, Marriage, and Family

Every human being has numerous identities, roles, and responsibilities, too many to mention. A person is a child or an adult, male or female, son or daughter, mother or father, single or married, young, middle-aged, or senior. Every station in life brings inescapable moral responsibilities involving one's sexuality and family status. A mother giving birth to a child sets in motion a whole series of obligations, starting with someone new to rear and love. For the household economy it means a new mouth to feed and another person to educate. For society it means another person to protect and defend according to the law, for the state another citizen and voting member. Christian theology has a long and profound tradition of ethical reflection and moral reasoning applicable to the ethics of sex, marriage, and family.

---

14. Matthew 25:35–36, 40.

The sixth commandment of the Decalogue, "You shall not commit adultery," has a broad relevance to every kind of unchastity in thought, word, and deed, and is not limited to the prohibition of sexual intercourse by either partner in violation of the marital vow of fidelity. This is clear from something Jesus said, "But I say to you that every one who looks at a woman lustfully has already committed adultery with her in his heart."[15] This is tantamount to agreeing with Paul, "None is righteous, no, not one. . . . All have sinned and fall short of the glory of God."[16] The Scriptures are clear about this: sex as such is not sinful. It cannot be; God created it and said it was good. "God created man in his own image, in the image of God created he him; male and female created he them. And God blessed them, and God said to them, 'Be fruitful and multiply, and fill the earth.'"[17] This is the biblical passage that upholds the integrity and dignity of human sexuality. God is love, and he revealed his image in two sexually different persons. Love implies a relationship between a lover and the beloved. God saw that it would not be good for man to live alone, because alone man cannot give and receive love. The human anatomy is so constructed as to exhibit the bi-polarity of the sexes. In the realm of nature there may always be anomalies that deviate from the norm, calling for understanding and compassion. Christian ethics affirms, nonetheless, that the sexual difference between male and female is God's original design for human life on planet earth.

Sexuality is a dimension of love that expresses itself in the "one flesh" union between a man and a woman. This love is so profound that Scripture uses it as analogous to the love of God for his people Israel and the love of Christ for his church. Sexuality is one but not the only dimension of human love. A married couple may continue to love each other long after the flame of sexual love has been extinguished by sickness or age. Love is a many-splendored thing; indeed, it is. *Libido* is a term made famous by Sigmund Freud, referring to the sexual drive derived from the id. This too has been created by God to draw a man and woman into a romantic relationship. Libido is also subject to the fallen human condition, expressing itself as an insatiable lust for pleasure for its own sake. This libidinous kind of sex degenerates into sinful perversions and social tragedies such as human trafficking, pornography, rape, incest, bestiality, and the like.

15. Matthew 5:28.
16. Romans 3:10, 23.
17. Genesis 1:27–28a.

Eros is a majestic sort of love that Plato used to express the human attraction to the inherent beauty and loveliness of someone or something. However, in ordinary language *eros* has come to mean romantic love between two persons. It can be fickle and fleeting, like falling in and out of love multiple times—Hollywood style. *Philia* is another type of love that Aristotle described in his book of ethics. It means the love between friends, the kind of love that David and Jonathan had for each other. The word *Philadelphia* means brotherly love; *philosophy* means the love of wisdom. *Libido, eros,* and *philia* are types of love that are unstable. Even the best of friends can have a falling out. There is another type of love at the heart of the biblical story of salvation, the *agapé* love of God. "God so '*agapéd*' the world that he gave his only Son, that whoever believes in him should not perish but have eternal life."[18] This is the forgiving, self-sacrificing, and passionate love of God expressed in the suffering of Christ on the cross. *Agapé* is unselfish, seeking the welfare of the other, quite the opposite of libido, which seeks only to gratify itself.

The four types of love, *libido, eros, philia,* and *agapé,* find their greatest fulfillment within the framework of a monogamous marriage and family life. The Christian view is that marriage is a union of one man and one woman. "Therefore, a man leaves his father and mother and cleaves to his wife, and they become one flesh."[19] Marriage is also an institution of society established by God in the order of creation, not an exclusively Christian phenomenon in the order of redemption. The state issues marriage licenses, the church does not. The facts of life are the same for all. However, for Christians marriage is a mystery—the love of Christ for his church is symbolized by the love between husband and wife.

> Husbands, love your wives, as Christ loved the church and gave himself up for her, that he might sanctify her, having cleansed her by the washing of water with the word, that the church might be presented before him in splendor, without spot or wrinkle or any such thing, that she might be holy and without blemish. Even so husbands should love their wives as their own bodies. He who loves his wife loves himself. For no man hates his own flesh, but nourishes it and cherishes it, as Christ does the church, because we are members of his body. For this reason a man shall leave his father and mother and be joined to his wife, and the two shall

18. John 3:16.
19. Genesis 2:24.

become one. This is a great mystery, and I take it to mean Christ and the church.[20]

This passage makes clear that the marital estate ordained by God in the order of creation is connected with the history of God's redemptive action in Christ. This connection has convinced the Roman Catholic Church to elevate marriage between the baptized to the dignity of a sacrament.[21] Even those who do not list marriage as one of the sacraments on the order of baptism and the Lord's Supper, since it was neither instituted by Christ nor is it a means of grace unto salvation, marriage may be accorded sacramental character as a sign of Christ's relation to his church.

According to God's design marriage is meant to be indissoluble, not a temporary convenience or arrangement to continue as long as love shall last. "The two shall become one. So they are no longer two but one. What therefore God has joined together, let no man put asunder."[22] The New Testament picture of marriage as a parable of Christ's love for his church presupposes that monogamy is God's intention, not polygamy or polyandry. Husband and wife are to be as devoted to each other as Christ is to his church.

Marriage is a vocation, a calling from God. In the Christian tradition celibacy has also been accepted as a divine calling. To elevate this calling the medieval church taught that virginity is superior to marriage, confirmed by the widespread belief that Mary, after the birth of Jesus, always remained a virgin (*semper virgine*). Luther also believed and taught this pious belief in the perpetual virginity of Mary, as also did Huldreich Zwingli and John Wesley,[23] even though all four Gospels refer to the "brothers and sisters" of Jesus. Four brothers were singled out by name—James, Joseph, Simon, and Judas.[24] Paul also referred to the "brothers of the Lord"[25] and to "James the Lord's brother."[26] Luther was a monk; he married a nun. Like many monks and priests who have tried the celibate lifestyle for religious reasons, Luther

---

20. Ephesians 5:25–32.
21. *Catechism of the Catholic Church*, 463.
22. Matthew 19: 5b–6.
23. Luther, "The Smalcald Articles," 292, 295.
24. See Matthew 12:46–49; 13:55–56; Mark 3:31–35; 6:3; Luke 8:19–20; John 2:12; 7:3–5.
25. 1 Corinthians 9:5.
26. Galatians 1:19.

probably finally felt he had to yield to the Apostle Paul's counsel, "It is better to marry than to be aflame with passion."[27]

The ultimate criterion of sexual activity is marriage. The Bible condemns all sorts of sexual behavior contrary to the divine imperative, "You shall not commit adultery." The list leaves virtually every person unscathed and without excuse—immorality, licentiousness, adultery, sodomy, homosexuality. These are part of a longer list including every imaginable kind of sinner who will not inherit the kingdom of God—murderers, kidnapers, liars, perjurers, idolaters, thieves, drunkards, revilers, slanderers, haters of God, as well as greedy, insolent, haughty, boastful, disobedient, foolish, heartless, and ruthless persons. Ergo: "All have sinned and fall short of the glory of God."[28] The apostolic message is the same for all: there is none righteous, no, not one; repent and believe in the gospel, and you will be saved [forgiven]; for sinners are saved by the gift of the grace of God through faith in Christ apart from works prescribed by the law. When Paul said he was the "chief of sinners," he was in effect saying that no sinner, no matter how great, is beyond redemption.

Questions for Discussion

1. What is the subject matter of theological ethics and why is it important for the Christian community and the daily life of individual Christians?
2. How is the doctrine of justification by faith relevant to ethics?
3. Do Christians have a responsibility for what is going on in the secular world of politics, business, labor, etc.? If so, why do some urge that religion and politics remain completely separate, especially in preaching?
4. Luther said he would rather be governed by a Turk than a corrupt Christian. What do you think he was trying to convey?
5. The Bible has a lot to say about money, wealth, rich people, and much of it includes dire warnings, even condemnations. In today's world there is a tremendous gap between the rich and the poor. Why should Christians care and what can they do about it?

27. 1 Corinthians 7:9b.
28. Romans 3:23.

11. THE CHURCH AND THE WORLD

6. The realm of "sex, marriage, and family" is part of God's created order; it is therefore subject to the civic laws that govern all people. What difference does the order of redemption make in how Christians understand and organize their lives within these universal institutions of creation?

7. *Agapé* is the uniquely biblical concept of love. What are its characteristics and how is it qualitatively different from the other types of love?

12. The Christian Mission and World Religions

A theology of the Christian mission in world history begins with the words Jesus spoke when he appeared to his disciples after his resurrection and before his ascension, "All authority in heaven and on earth has been given to me. Go therefore and make disciples of all nations, baptizing them in the name of the Father and of the Son and of the Holy Spirit, teaching them to observe all that I have commanded you; and lo, I am with you always, to the close of the age."[1] Millions of Christians have taken these words literally, crossing every frontier to baptize in the name of the triune God and teaching the gospel of Christ to people in every country, of all races and cultures, and in every language and dialect. Christianity began with a handful of witnesses of the risen Jesus in Jerusalem two thousand-some years ago. The conviction that "He is risen" resounded among the first believers in Jesus as the Messiah, convincing them that this eschatological truth cannot be confined to the Jews but must be shouted to all peoples.

Today the Christian religion numbers more than two billion adherents, is the world's largest religious group, and a third of the world's population. Courageous and devoted evangelists and missionaries following in the footsteps of the apostles have made that happen. Jesus said that just as he was sent by his Father, so he is sending his followers into the world.[2] This pattern of "sending and going" started with the call of Abraham. God sent Abraham and he went; he sent Joseph and he went; he sent Moses and he went. Isaiah "heard the voice of the Lord saying, 'Whom shall I send, and who will go for us?' Then I said, 'Here I am! Send me.'"[3] The Apostle Paul wrote, "But how are men to call upon him in whom they have not believed?

---

1. Matthew 28:19–20.
2. John 20:21.
3. Isaiah 6:8.

12. THE CHRISTIAN MISSION AND WORLD RELIGIONS

And how are they to believe in him of whom they have never heard? And how are they to hear without a preacher? And how can men preach unless they are sent? As it is written, 'How beautiful are the feet of those who preach good news!'"[4] Passages such as these have been the marching orders of millions of "called and sent" missionaries of the gospel to places far and near. Many have lived to tell their stories that matched Paul's on his missionary journeys—imprisoned, shipwrecked, robbed and beaten, cold and sleepless, hungry and thirsty.[5] Many more have not survived; statistics indicate that the number of missionaries martyred for bearing witness to Christ has increased greatly in modern times, behind the Iron and Bamboo curtains, for example, and in Muslim and Hindu societies that forbid any sort of evangelistic and missionary activity.[6]

In Christianity today there are many doubting Thomases who question the validity of the Christian mission to the non-Christian world. Christian leaders who no longer believe in world evangelization, that is, the attempt to invite people of other religions or no religion at all to become believers in Christ and members of his church, are redefining mission to mean something else, using terms such as *humanization, development,* and *liberation,* and launching programs to combat racism, poverty, hunger, malaria, and to promote equality, freedom, peace, and justice. These are all worthy matters of social responsibility that Christians are called by God to support. In fact, Christians are mandated to be the vanguard of God's mission to expand freedom, equality, and justice in all aspects and areas of society. But doing these things are not the mission Jesus had in mind when he told his followers to go and tell his gospel to those who do not believe. Every serious Christian missionary effort has accompanied its preaching of the gospel with educational, agricultural, and medical programs to improve the lives of people.

Ecumenism and Mission

The ecumenical commitment to the worldwide evangelistic mission of the church is based on some core beliefs of New Testament Christianity. First, Jesus assured the disciples of John the Baptist that he is the long-awaited

4. Romans 10:14–15.
5. 2 Corinthians 11:23–27.
6. Hinlicky and Nelson, *Martyrdom and the Suffering of the Righteous.*

Messiah, so there is no need to look for another.[7] Second, faith in Jesus Christ means personal participation in the reality of salvation achieved through his death and resurrection. Third, it is God's desire to save all people and bring them to the knowledge of the truth.[8] Fourth, God has entrusted the church with the task to proclaim the apostolic gospel to all peoples between the times of his first and final advent.

No one denomination has the resources to carry out the universal mission of the gospel by itself. The modern ecumenical movement has taken to heart the prayer of Jesus "that they may all be one . . . that the world might believe."[9] They share the conviction that "the whole church is to bring the whole gospel to the whole world." Evangelicals, mainline Protestants, Roman Catholics, and Eastern Orthodox have contributed to an ecumenical manifesto entitled *Mission and Evangelism—An Ecumenical Affirmation*. This document expresses a gratifying convergence of belief that all humanity is in need of the salvation that God has wrought in the life, death, and resurrection of Jesus Christ and that Christ has commissioned his church to reach all peoples of the world with the message of the gospel. The convictions of this ecumenical document are reinforced by the papal encyclical of John Paul II, *Ut Unum Sint*. It affirms that evangelization today must be done in tandem with full ecumenical cooperation, that the world may know "that the love with which thou [the Father] hast loved me [Jesus] may be in them, and I in them."[10] The encyclical asks, "How can we proclaim the gospel of reconciliation without at the same time being committed to working for reconciliation between Christians?"[11] The Pope's encyclical goes on to state, "Believers in Christ . . . cannot remain divided. . . . How could they refuse to do everything possible . . . to overcome obstacles and prejudices which thwart the proclamation of the Gospel of salvation in the cross of Jesus?"[12] The encyclical acknowledges that ecumenical cooperation in world evangelization requires a common faith and right teaching. Heresies divide and result in schisms. "The unity willed by God can be attained only by the

---

7. Matthew 11:3.
8. 1 Timothy 1:4.
9. John 17:21.
10. John 17:26.
11. John Paul II, *Ut Unum Sint*, 98,
12. John Paul II, *Ut Unum Sint*, 1, 2.

adherence of all to the content of the revealed faith in its entirety. In matters of faith, compromise is in contradiction with God who is Truth."[13]

The unity willed by God does not mean uniformity of doctrinal emphasis in every respect. Each of the denominations typically brings a particular aspect of biblical Christianity to expression. Cooperation in mission and evangelism need not expunge the polyphonic riches the denominations bring to the ecumenical roundtable. Anglicans bring a theology of the incarnation, Lutherans a theology of the cross, the Orthodox a theology of the resurrection, Calvinists a focus on the ascension, Adventists emphasize the future parousia, Pentecostals the empowerment of the Holy Spirit. An ecumenical strategy brings to the fields of mission the fullness of the classical Christian tradition, so that the younger churches are freed from the tendency to be carbon copies of the particular theological emphasis of their founding denomination.

The Christian mission to evangelize the nations is motivated by what St. Peter, filled with the Holy Spirit, preached to the ruling elders of Jerusalem after Pentecost: "There is salvation in no one else, for there is no other name under heaven given among mortals by which we must be saved."[14] This conviction is reinforced by the Apostle Paul's warning, something modern Christians need to hear as much as those first century Galatians:

> I am astonished that you are so quickly deserting him who called you in the grace of Christ and turning to a different gospel—not that there is another gospel, but there are some who trouble you and want to pervert the gospel of Christ. But even if we, or an angel from heaven, would preach to you a gospel contrary to that which we preached to you, let him be accursed. As we have said before, so now I say again, If anyone is preaching to you a gospel contrary to that which you received, let him be accursed.[15]

The Pluralistic Theory of Religions

Ever since the Enlightenment the Christian missionary endeavor to reach the nations has faced strong headwinds of criticism by a pluralistic theory

---

13. John Paul II, *Ut Unum Sint*, 18.
14. Acts 4:12.
15. Galatians 1:6–9.

of religions touting a different gospel. This "enlightened" gospel is the good news that there are many saviors of humanity, enough to go around for everyone, with no need to hear a word about Christ. All religions are equally salvific. Christianity suffers from the old-fashioned myth, it is averred, that its gospel of Christ is uniquely and exclusively true. That is why it believes it has something special to export to the nations. The chorus of voices has reached a crescendo, "Missionary, go home!" Many churches have brought their missionaries home, handing a Pyrrhic victory to the ideology of religious pluralism. When all the "one and only" exclusive particles of Christology and the gospel are surrendered, there remains only the simplistic counsel that people should adhere to their own religions and learn how to be pious and moral as each of them inculcates in its own members.

Gotthold Ephraim Lessing (1729–1781) was a leading philosopher of the Enlightenment. He told a story about a certain father who had three sons. It was the custom for the father to give his favorite son a special ring that had the magic power to make him beloved of God and humanity. But this father loved all three sons equally. To please all of them he made two imitations of the special ring. Before he died he gave each son a ring with his blessing. Each of the sons believed he had the true ring and considered the others false. The three sons wanted to find out which of them had the special ring. So they went to a wise judge, Nathan. Nathan offered his counsel: Let each one of you think his own ring is the real one and trust that in a thousand thousand years the true ring will prove itself by the "proof of the spirit and power." Meanwhile, he said, let each son show forth a spirit of tolerance and gentleness to the others.[16]

This message of enlightened reason will supposedly bring peace among the nations and the religious wars will cease. The problem is that every religion other than Christian may be content to hear that Judaism is for Jews, Islam is for Muslims, Hinduism is for Hindus, Buddhism is for Buddhists, etc., but for Christianity it is a recipe for suicidal extinction. If the first apostles would have followed the pluralistic hypothesis, Christianity would have remained a Palestinian sect. Paul would not have taken the gospel to the Gentiles, who for the most part did not issue the Macedonian call, "Come over and help us."[17] Within one generation there would have been no Ro-

---

16. Lessing, *Nathan the Wise*.
17. Acts 16:9.

12. THE CHRISTIAN MISSION AND WORLD RELIGIONS

man or Greek Christians. Except for all the missionaries who followed Paul's example, there would be no Christian church in Ireland or Iceland, no Christians in Scandinavia or Russia, no Christians in South Africa or South America, etc. Those are simply world-historical facts that cannot be refuted. Paul's reminder bears repeating, "There is no other gospel than the one he received from Jesus and his apostles, and if anyone preaches a different gospel, let him be damned."[18]

On the other hand, the Christian missionary movement in world history would have benefited from Nathan's advice to show a "spirit of tolerance and gentleness to the others," given the spotty record of imperial Christendom too often exhibiting a crusading spirit of arrogance, superiority, triumphalism, colonialism, apartheid, and the like. This is in dire contradiction to the New Testament portrayal of Jesus whom God elected to be a "maker of peace by his blood on the cross."[19] The apostolic benediction announces, "The peace of God, which passes all understanding, will keep your hearts and your minds in Christ Jesus."[20] Or in the words of Paul's favorite: "Grace to you and peace from God our Father and the Lord Jesus Christ."[21] It is incumbent on missionary praxis to demonstrate that the Christian gospel is a message of peace and reconciliation. It is an obscene scandal every time Christians and their churches bless the unjust wars fought by the nations of which they are citizens.

Even though the pluralistic theory of religions is unacceptable from a theological perspective normed by the New Testament gospel of Christ, that does not mean that Christianity is inimical to pluralism as such, as though a monomorphic expression of religion is more to be favored. The catholicity of the church embraces a variety of religious expressions, shaped by the pluralities of human experience having to do with gender, age, language, race, culture, and ethnicity. Pentecost was a pluralistic phenomenon, experienced by "Parthians and Medes and Elamites and residents of Mesopotamia, Judea and Cappadocia, Pontus and Asia, Phrygia and Pamphylia, Egypt and the parts of Libya, belonging to Cyrene, and visitors from Rome,

18. Galatians 1:6–9.
19. Colossians 1:20.
20. Philippians 4:7.
21. Romans 1:4; 1 Corinthians 1:3; 2 Corinthians 1:2; Galatians 1:3; Ephesians 1:2; Philippians 1:2.

both Jews and proselytes, Cretans and Arabians, we hear them telling in their own tongues the mighty works of God."[22] All these people came to their Pentecostal experience in Jerusalem from a variety of religious backgrounds. They already knew something about what God had revealed to them. Paul and Barnabas said to the Greeks in Lystra that God did "not leave himself without witness."[23] In writing to the Romans Paul taught that God had revealed something of himself prior to and apart from his saving revelation in Christ Jesus: "Ever since the creation of the world his invisible nature, namely, his eternal power and deity, has been clearly perceived in the things that have been made."[24] Paul preached in Athens in the middle of the Areopagus, "Athenians, I perceive that in every way you are very religious. . . . For he is not far from each one of us, for 'in him we live, and move, and have our being.'"[25]

Preparation for the Gospel

In St. Paul's theology the law is understood as preparation for the gospel, not annulled by it. The law accuses, the gospel forgives. The religions too are not nullified but each in its own way is a preparation for the missionary proclamation of the gospel. When religious persons become Christians through faith and baptism, they invariably testify that they have found the fulfillment rather than the negation of all they experienced of truth, beauty, and goodness in their previous religious life. Augustine was a Platonist before his conversion to Christ. In his *Confessions* he acknowledged how much he learned from Platonic philosophy. He learned about the Logos that John's Gospel says was a co-creator with the Father, the author of life, the light that shines in darkness, and the true light that enlightens every human soul.[26] But that the Word became flesh is not something he learned from philosophy or religion, but only from the Scriptures and the church.

Adolf von Harnack wrote five volumes on the history of Christianity in which he tracked what he called the "Hellenization of the gospel." When the gospel left Jerusalem and went west to Greece, Rome, North Africa,

22. Acts 2:9–11.
23. Acts 1:17.
24. Romans 1:20.
25. Acts 17: 22, 17b, 28.
26. John 1:1–3.

12. THE CHRISTIAN MISSION AND WORLD RELIGIONS

and throughout Europe, it assumed the accents, idioms, and styles of their indigenous religions and cultures. Harnack said Christianity was "Hellenized" when it used Greek philosophical terms to express its faith and doctrines. Another way to express this idea is to say that Christianity is a syncretistic religion. This idea might seem to threaten the uniqueness of the Christian message. To the contrary, that has proven to be its strength. The missionary encounter of Christianity and the religions gives numerous examples of the syncretistic process, while at the same time maintaining the truth of the gospel that the God revealed in Jesus Christ is identical with the God at work in all the religions other than Christian. Something unique and definitive happened in the history and message of Jesus. That "something" is the final revelation of the God of Israel in Jesus who is the alpha of creation and the omega of redemption.

The Great Tradition of classical Christianity followed Paul and virtually all the church fathers in teaching a universal revelation of God discernible in all nations, cultures, and religions. When missionaries translated the Bible and preached the gospel to people of other religions, they discovered that God was already known and addressed by many different names, but that did not detract from their message that his gift of salvation, forgiveness of sin, and liberation from bondage, is on account of Christ alone. Every religion offers its devotees some kind of deliverance from what it perceives as the fundamental human predicament. Such deliverance varies from religion to religion, be it illumination, unification, immortality, or liberation. There are different synonyms for salvation in the New Testament—reconciliation, justification, redemption, atonement, forgiveness of sins, adoption, and eternal life. What matters is that each metaphor is a function of the person and work of Christ. "There is salvation in no one else, for there is no other name under heaven given among mortals by which we must be saved."[27]

Interpretation of Religions Other Than Christian

Jews and Muslims and Hindus and Buddhists have a positive appreciation of Jesus as a teacher, prophet, and moral example. Modern dialogues between Jews and Christians have helped Christians to rediscover their Hebrew roots, after centuries of Hellenization. Jewish scholars are reclaiming Jesus as one of them. They come from the same household of faith and

27. Acts 4:12.

share the same sacred Scriptures. They can take pride that Christians also claim Abraham as their father, that so many Gentiles place their trust in a Jewish Messiah, and that Jesus prayed to the same "Abba" as they do. And Christians for their part do not lose hope for the salvation that God has in store for his chosen people. "I want you to understand this mystery, brethren, a hardening has come upon a part of Israel, until the full number of the Gentiles come in, and so all Israel will be saved."[28] Paul explains how that can that be: "For the gifts and the call of God are irrevocable."[29] Jews will continue to pray for the coming of the Messiah; Christians pray to the Messiah who has already come. The separation between Jews and Christians is a matter of timing, a real difference now, but one that will some day be overcome.[30]

Islam

The sacred book of Islam, the Qu'ran, contains explicit teaching about Jesus of Nazareth whom Muslims revere as a prophet and messenger of Allah, even a suffering servant of God. The Qu'ran speaks of Jesus as the Word and Truth of God, in the line of the great Hebrew prophets from Moses to David. The Qu'ran shares other Christian beliefs about Jesus, including his resurrection and ascension into heaven. Muslims are radical monotheists; they reject the doctrine of the Trinity, because they disbelieve that Jesus is the Son of God, of one being with the Father. The Qu'ran is aware that Christians believe in the three persons of the Godhead, which it condemns as unbelief. The Qu'ran says, "They are unbelievers who say that God is threefold. No god there is but one God."

Do Christians and Muslims pray to the same God? Do they believe in the same way of salvation? In many parts of the world Muslims and Christians have entered into dialogue, searching for mutually respectful answers to these and other similar questions. In other parts of the world the ancient conflicts between Muslims and non-Muslim countries continue, breaking out into violence and war. Both Christianity and Islam claim to be religions of peace, and both have failed miserably to find ways to express it. Where Christians are in the majority, they respect the right of Muslims to practice

---

28. Romans 11:25–26a.
29. Romans 11:29.
30. Qu'ran, Sur 5, 78.

and propagate their faith. Where Muslims are in the majority, Christianity is treated as an outlaw religion with no right to proclaim the gospel, to build churches, and to worship in public.

Hinduism

According to tradition, St. Thomas the Apostle brought Christianity to India and founded the church named after him, the St. Thomas Christian Church. There are roughly thirty million Christians in India, less than 3 percent of the population. Despite its minority status Christianity contributes to Indian society with its many educational institutions and hospitals. Hinduism is the major religion. In many parts of India Hindus and Christians enjoy amicable relations.

Mahatma Ghandi (1869–1948) was a Hindu religious, political, and social reformer, and leader of the passive resistance movement that gained independence for India from British rule. He said he was inspired by the message of Jesus: "It is the Sermon on the Mount that endeared Jesus to me. . . . Although I cannot claim to be a Christian in a confessional sense, still the example of Jesus' suffering is a factor in the make-up of the fundamental belief in non-violence that guides all my worldly and temporary actions."[31] Yet, in spite of the favorable image of Jesus in India, Christian evangelization faces strong religious opposition in some parts of India. Anti-Christian violence has flared up in recent decades; churches have been burned, and missionaries have been martyred. Conversion from Hinduism to Christianity is not only politically difficult but also religiously discouraged by the fact that Hinduism can tolerate a plurality of deities, including the figure of Christ, in its pantheon, along with Krishna, Rama, Isvara, Purusha, and others. Jesus may be accepted as one among many "avataras" or incarnations of a supreme Reality. Young Hindu missionaries are visible in airports selling their sacred books, the Upanishads or the Bhagavadgita.

---

31. Quoted by Küng, *Christianity and World Religions*, 282.

Buddhism

Due to the influence of Thomas Merton and the Dalai Lama, Christians and Buddhists have entered into interfaith dialogues, conducted in a spirit of openness and mutual respect. Similarities and differences are readily recognized and acknowledged, beginning with their respective founders. Buddha is the enlightened one, Jesus is the anointed one. Buddha was born 567 BC into a life of luxury. Jesus was born the son of a carpenter. As a young man Buddha opted for an ascetic life of poverty. Buddha and Jesus were both itinerant preachers with a message of salvation. Both of them had disciples and taught by means of parables and proverbs. Both of them were severe critics of the established authorities, especially the priests of their religions. Both of them called for a change of heart and mind, with a total commitment to an alternative way of life. Both of them were critical of living in pursuit of wealth and riches, giving absolute loyalty to matters of relative value. There have been attempts to syncretize the two religions, as far back as the Nestorians in the fifth century, but without much success. The chief reason is that Christians and Buddhists are related to their respective founders in fundamentally different ways.

To be a Christian is to believe in Jesus as the Son of God, as one's personal Lord and Savior, and the eschatological fulfillment of the spiritual quest occurring in all religions. To be a Buddhist is to accept some basic ideas and tenets that Buddha taught and to engage regularly in practices, such as meditation, to curb the longing and craving that cause human suffering and dissatisfaction. In Christianity salvation is by the grace of God, not by the practices of piety or good works. Grace is a free gift of God. In Buddhism salvation (satisfaction) is by works prescribed to end unhappiness, something that humans do by following the right path. In Christianity the central figure of faith is the man hanging on a cross, the price Jesus paid for bringing in the kingdom of God's universal love. In Buddhism the central figure is sitting on a lotus blossom, smiling and feeling good and tranquil. The cross of Christ is the chief point of difference between the Christian way of salvation and all other religious systems. Paul called the crucified Christ the foolishness of God, a stumbling-block to Jews and folly to Gentiles.[32]

---

32. 1 Corinthians 1:20–25.

12. THE CHRISTIAN MISSION AND WORLD RELIGIONS

Insisting on the particularity of the gospel as the way of salvation seems to rule out the universality of God's will unto salvation. Theologians have debated the question whether God's will to save the whole fallen world through the redemption accomplished in Christ will be realized or frustrated in the end. There is no one dogmatic answer to this question. The common Christian belief is that the revelation of God in Jesus Christ is the eschatological fulfillment of the religions of humankind. The universality of Christ is expressed through the interaction of the religions in world history and will be vindicated for all eyes to see only at the end of history. The future is still outstanding. This means that the final destiny of those who do not believe in Christ in their lifetime is a mystery about which theologians have speculated. The Christian church has not been given a transcript or video of what God will decide at the last judgment. Paul has given Christians a word about which they are to think and do in the meantime.

> To me, though I am the very least of all the saints, this grace was given, to preach to the Gentiles the unsearchable riches of Christ, and to make all men see what is the plan of the mystery hidden for ages in God who created all things; that through the church the manifold wisdom of God might now be made known to the principalities and powers in the heavenly places. This was to the eternal purpose which he has realized in Christ Jesus our Lord, in whom we have boldness and confidence of access through our faith in him.[33]

Eschatology is the proper locus of dogmatics that deals with the end times, the Great Transformation of all things at the end of history, including the pros and cons of universal salvation.

Questions for Discussion

1. What is the biblical basis for the Christian evangelistic mission to the world?

2. Some churches have never been committed to the world missionary movement and evangelization. Some churches today seem to be more interested in issues of world peace and justice. If you were in charge of church planning and administration, what would you propose as the priorities of the church?

---

33. Ephesians 3:8–12.

3. What does the ecumenical concern for the unity of the church have to do with Jesus' missional command to "preach the gospel to all the nations"?

4. Acts 4:12 states, "There is salvation in no one else, for there is no other name under heaven given among mortals by which we must be saved." But there are many gods with many names in the universe of the world's religions. What is the significance of that biblical passage relative to what Christians and churches should believe and do today?

5. God has revealed something of his will to all people. There is general or natural revelation, apart from God's special revelation in the Bible. How should you describe the essential difference between those two forms of revelation?

6. The pluralistic theory of religions may now be the majority view of how the religions relate to each other in the modern world. If the church of the first five centuries and thereafter would have acted on that theory, what do you think would be the state of world Christianity today?

7. How does Christianity relate to Judaism from a biblical theological point of view? How is that relationship different from the way it relates to other religions, especially Islam, Hinduism, and Buddhism?

13. Eschatology: The Christian Hope

Eschatology is the doctrine that concerns the final aim of human life and the world beyond death and annihilation. Christian eschatology is based on the hope that on account of Jesus' resurrection from the dead God will recreate new life beyond the world we now experience. The inescapable question is whether such a hope is well-founded on truth and reality. The answer to this question is based on the trustworthiness of the entire revelation of God transmitted by the Holy Scriptures. Christian eschatological hope for life beyond death is deeply anchored in the biblical depiction of the God of Israel as a God of history and hope. The Apostle Paul retells the story of Abraham as a journey of hope, of hoping beyond hope, "when hope seemed hopeless."[1] Paul makes clear that the Christian gospel of hope engendered by the resurrection of Jesus is adumbrated by the promise of God to Abraham.

> As it is written, "I have made you the father of many nations"—in the presence of God in whom he believed, who gives life to the dead and calls into existence the things that do not exist. . . . No distrust made him waver concerning the promise of God, but he grew strong in his faith as he gave glory to God, fully convinced that God was able to do what he had promised. That is why his faith was "reckoned to him as righteousness." But the words, "it was reckoned to him," were written not for his sake alone, but for ours also. It will be reckoned to us who believe in him that raised from the dead Jesus our Lord, who was put to death for our trespasses and raised for our justification.[2]

The core of eschatological hope for a future beyond death is faith in God. Faith in God and hope for the future of life are like two horses pulling the

---

1. Romans 4:18.
2. Romans 4:17, 20–25.

same chariot. Biblical faith and hope are experientially interdependent. The Old Testament prologue to New Testament eschatology continues after Abraham with the story of Moses. Moses led the Israelites on an exodus out of oppression and slavery in Egypt toward the promised land "flowing with milk and honey."[3] On the way to the future of God's promise is manna sufficient for the day. Moses had to deal with a double threat, first, that of growing weary with hope, seeking satisfaction in the present while dancing around a golden calf, and second, that of despairing of the promised future, yearning instead to go back to the fleshpots of Egypt. Such threats could only be overcome by faith in God who named himself, *"Eh'je ascher eh'je,"* translated by biblical scholars as "I will be who I will be"—a God with power to bring about the future of hope for deliverance from evil and liberation from bondage.

As the story of Israel unfolds in the Hebrew Scriptures (Old Testament) the phenomenon of hope is expanded to embrace not only Israel's future but also that of all nations. And in later apocalyptic literature hope includes the final destiny of the whole universe. The Lordship of God is proclaimed over all nations and all things, and his judgment is pronounced against all demonic powers that challenge his supreme authority. Death itself is viewed as the chief enemy of humanity. But the Old Testament does not offer a sufficient reason for hope in the encounter with death. It leaves a blank that waits to be filled with the rise of hope for resurrection in later Judaism. When the apostles preached the resurrection of Jesus, they were announcing the dawning of the eschatological future of God's kingdom.

The ensuing belief that "Jesus is risen" became the core of the apostolic message that God "desires all people to be saved and come to the knowledge of the truth."[4] It is the task of eschatology to explicate the Christian hope for eternal communion with God, not only for a handful of believers here and now but for all human persons and all things, through Christ, "For in him all the fullness of God was pleased to dwell, and through him to reconcile to himself all things, whether on earth or in heaven, making peace by the blood of the cross."[5] Every limit to the universality of God's redemptive plan for the world is negated in this passage. The universal promise of

---

3. Exodus 3:8.
4. 1 Timothy 2:4.
5. Colossians 1:20.

eschatological salvation has not yet been and will not be realized in world history. For when the kingdom of God arrives in its fullness, perfect justice and lasting peace will occur in full measure. Eschatological hope is not utopian. Utopia is a word derived from two Greek words, "*ou*" meaning "not" and "*topos*," meaning place. There is literally no place on earth where individuals and communities exist in perfect harmony with each other and in communion with their eternal Creator. Nevertheless, the biblical prophets envisioned a future in which all the nations of the earth will come to Mount Zion and have their conflicts and rights adjudicated by God, so they may enjoy permanent peace and real justice in the historical future.

The New Testament is more realistic and harbors no such utopian hopes. The kingdom of God will not be fully realized "on earth as it is in heaven," that is, sometime in the distant this-worldly future. The kingdom of God will not come about by human action, social engineering, or political schemes. Nor will it be founded on earth by Christians based on Christian principles and governed by Christian rulers with the best intentions to create a perfect society. However, hope for the coming of God's kingdom at the end of history can inspire Christian action and stimulate efforts to create a better world in the meantime.

Resurrection of the Dead

Belief in the bodily resurrection of the dead has been a part of Christian eschatology every since the apostles began to preach the gospel of Jesus Christ. Paul declared that the physical body will be replaced by a spiritual body (*soma pneumatikos*).[6] This belief was ridiculed by the Greek philosophical intelligentsia. Plotinus is reported as saying he was ashamed of having a body. "The true philosopher is entirely concerned with the soul and not the body. He would like, as far as he can, to get away from the body."[7] This is opposite the Christian affirmation of the body. Paul wrote, "The body is a temple of the Holy Spirit."[8] Both Christians and their pagan neighbors believed in life after death. For Christians it meant resurrection of the whole person, body and soul; for non-Christians it meant immortality of the soul without a body.

6. 1 Corinthians 15:42–44.
7. Quoted by Owen, *Body and Soul*, 39.
8. 1 Corinthians 6:19.

It is a long story, but Christian theology eventually made a compromise with the Greek philosophical idea of immortality of the soul. Both medieval Catholic and Protestant scholastic theology constructed a synthesis of the biblical concept of resurrection and the Greek philosophical idea of immortality. And that synthesis continues unabated and unrevised in virtually all branches of modern Christianity—Orthodox, Catholic, and Protestant. Funeral sermons console mourners that death is merely the end of a person's physical life on earth; it does not spell total annihilation. The soul of the deceased survives the death of the body, and has moved on to another place, usually unspecified. Some speculated that the soul lingers on in a state of sleep until it is reunited with its resurrected body to face the final judgment when God will welcome the saved into heavenly bliss and condemn the lost to eternal hellfire. Protestants shed the medieval Catholic ideas of purgatory and limbo, but otherwise retained the basic elements of the amalgamated eschatology of scholastic theology.

Rethinking Traditional Eschatology

According to the medieval scheme of eschatology, the final judgment immediately follows the resurrection of the dead, and when that takes place, the world will come to an end. The world will be annihilated in a ball of fire. The whole human and natural world created by God will be split in two, one part headed for hell, eternal damnation and endless misery, keeping company with the devil and all the fallen angels, and another part destined for eternity, a glorious and beautiful life, feeling no need for food, drink, or sex.

The medieval scholastic eschatology is based on a literal interpretation of biblical apocalyptic images and symbols mixed with heterogenous ideas stemming from Greek philosophy and gnostic speculation. Modern systematic theologians have reappropriated biblical eschatology,[9] no longer beholden to the traditional dogmatics of Roman Catholic Tridentine[10] and seventeenth-century Protestant orthodoxy.[11] Yet, present-day rethinking of eschatology

---

9. For example, Karl Barth, Paul Tillich, Karl Rahner, Wolfhart Pannenberg, and Jürgen Moltmann. As different as they are in many respects, none of them repristinates the eschatological systems of pre-Enlightenment theologies.

10. Referring to the decrees and doctrines of the Roman Catholic Council of Trent (1555–1565).

11. Cf. Schmid, *Doctrinal Theology of the Evangelical Lutheran Church*. This is a

has yielded a rich variety of schools of thought that lack consensus, coherence, and consistency. Any new attempt to construct a system of eschatology is likely to be eclectic, as this one is, given the fact that, on the one hand, twentieth-century theologians took seriously the rediscovery of eschatology in the teachings of Jesus, the New Testament as a whole, and early Christianity and, on the other hand, the realization that so much rethinking needed to be done to free Christian theology from a lot of accumulated baggage unreformed by the gracious gospel of Jesus Christ.

It is to the lasting credit of Albert Schweitzer (1875–1965), Alsatian missionary to West Africa, that as a young scholar he wrote a monumental work, *The Quest of the Historical Jesus*, in which he demonstrated that the message of Jesus was through and through eschatological, over against the reduction of his teachings to ethics and moral principles by liberal Protestant theologians.[12] Schweitzer showed that everything in Jesus' ministry of word and deed can be best explained in light of his expectation of the imminent coming of God's rule on earth. Schweitzer's view is commonly called "consistent eschatology," to express his scholarly conviction that everything the Gospels report about Jesus' life and teachings can be understood only in light of eschatology.

Karl Barth (1886–1968) took Schweitzer's thesis seriously. He launched his eminent theological career with his commentary on Paul's Epistle to the Romans, insisting that "Christianity that is not entirely and altogether eschatology has entirely and altogether nothing to do with Christ."[13] In this early stage of his career Barth held that eschatology does not refer to far distant things piling up at the end of history—the final judgment, the resurrection of the dead, the second coming of Christ—traditionally relegated to the last chapter of dogmatics. Eschatology is all about the eternal Word of God descending vertically from above, manifest in the incarnation of Jesus Christ. This view is commonly called "dialectical eschatology," because it hinges on the relation of eternity and time.

---

compendium of dogmatic statements of sixteenth- and seventeenth-century orthodox Lutheran theologians.

12. Schweitzer, *The Quest of the Historical Jesus*.
13. Barth, *Epistle to the Romans*, 314.

The revision of eschatology after Schweitzer continued to explore facets of the New Testament picture of Christ and the first expressions of the Christian faith. C. H. Dodd (1884–1973), a Welsh New Testament theologian, is known for teaching "realized eschatology." Whereas Schweitzer's view emphasized the imminent *future* of God's approaching kingdom, Dodd stressed that the kingdom of God had already arrived and was actively present in Jesus' ministry. Jesus said, "The Kingdom of God is in the midst of you."[14] Dodd disagreed with Schweitzer's eschatological hypothesis only with respect to the temporal factor, that is, whether the kingdom of God in Jesus' message and ministry was still future, although near, or already present with immediate urgency and efficacy.

Another significant view was proposed by Oscar Cullmann (1902–1999), modifying Dodd's hypothesis.[15] He agreed that the kingdom of God has already arrived in Jesus' words and actions, but there still remains more to be realized in the future. Cullmann's view is called "*Heilsgeschichte* eschatology,"[16] indicating that although the biblical story of salvation is about real events already occurring in world history, its end and fulfillment remain as objects of hope yet to be realized.

A view polar opposite "*Heislgeschichte* eschatology," whose strength lies in taking history seriously, is the "existentialist eschatology" of Rudolf Bultmann (1884–1976).[17] For Bultmann eschatology does not refer to an objective future end of history. Eschatology has to do with the present moment of existence in which God is calling for a critical decision to be or not to be, for life or for death, for faith or for futility. Existence in faith is eschatological; it is experienced as the forgiveness of sins through the preaching of the gospel (*kerygma*) of Christ. The New Testament references to the future in which the drama of redemption will come to completion at the end of history are demythologized, that is, reinterpreted to refer to existential possibilities of existence here and now. Everything future is swallowed up into the present moment of existence.

---

14. Luke 17:21.
15. Cullmann, *Christ and Time*.
16. *Heilsgeschichte* is a German word meaning "history of salvation."
17. Bultmann, *History and Eschatology*.

13. ESCHATOLOGY: THE CHRISTIAN HOPE

Each of the models of eschatology considered above conveys a truth to be affirmed; at the same time each is deficient in what it neglects. Schweitzer is right to stress that the future time dimension is implied when Jesus preached, "Repent, for the kingdom of heaven is at hand."[18] The phrase "at hand" means that soon (but not yet) the kingdom of God would be ushered in by a catastrophic judgment, followed by a victorious redemption. Barth is right to link eschatology to the Word of God incarnate. No talk about the world's future has any Christian relevance unless it is seen as a function of God's revelation in Jesus Christ. Yet, this true insight need not collapse the real future of Christ and history into a dialectic of eternity and time. Dodd is right in affirming that the parables and miracles of Jesus show that God's sovereign rule is already present and active in his ministry. However, it is equally true that the dynamics of eschatology continue in force after the death and resurrection of Christ, signaled by the outpouring of the Spirit at Pentecost and Christ's commission to his disciples to preach the eschatological gospel of God to all the nations. The *Heilsgechichte* eschatology of Cullmann is right to identify both the present and future aspects of the kingdom of God in the words and works of Jesus recorded in the Gospels and in the missionary activity of the first Christians narrated in the book of Acts. Cullmann refused to collapse the future of the kingdom in history into the existential moment of decision. However, there is good reason to question Cullmann's understanding of the history of salvation that places eschatology at the far end of history, for this would entail a quantitative view of eternity as endless time, thus failing to observe the qualitative distinction between time and eternity. It is more difficult to think of any redeeming aspect of Rudolf Bultmann's existentialist eschatology. The problem is that he has demythologized eschatology to the point that eschatology is reduced to the Lutheran soteriological doctrine of justification by faith. The forgiveness of sins proclaimed through the kerygma is the eschatological event. The only eschaton is the existential moment in which a decision for life or death is made. In his Gifford Lectures Bultmann addressed the question of the meaning of life. He said, "Do not look around yourself into universal history; you must look into your own personal history. Always in your present lies the meaning in history, and you cannot see it as a spectator, but only in your responsible decisions. In every moment slumbers the possibility of being the eschatological moment. You must awaken it."[19] In his view

18. Matthew 4:17.
19. Bultmann, *History and Eschatology*, 155.

eschatology has nothing to do with the history of redemption that will be consummated in the final drama of the coming of Christ to judge the living and the dead. Everything else is written off as relics of late Jewish apocalypticism, no longer relevant to how each individual stands before God.

One thing the various eschatological scenarios have in common is the irreducible Christian belief that Christ is the hope of the world and the Savior of every individual person. All are radically christocentric, even Bultmann's, no matter whether they do or do not do justice to the various time dimensions of history and eschatology. This accounts for the fact that the gospel of Jesus Christ can be preached within the framework of all the interpretive models surveyed above.

Hope and Universal Salvation

Eschatology is essential to a full treatment of Christian dogmatics. Certain methodological principles need to be observed to do justice to such a controversial and complicated subject. Eschatological statements in Christian theology and preaching make sense only when they are existentially relevant to what Christians think and do in their daily lives (giving Bultmann his due). Eschatological statements must reflect the biblical account of God's revealing word and redemptive work in and for the world from the beginning of creation, through the history of Israel, and the apostolic mission of the church to the nations, going forward in universal history in anticipation of the end when God will wrap things up and be all in all. Eschatological statements must be christocentric, because Christ is the mediator between God and the world; he is the future of the world and of every human person. Eschatological statements need to address the future of what is going on in the world and of all persons, because that is where all of us will spend the rest of our lives, whether in view of the horizontal future in this life or the vertical future beyond death to a new everlasting life with God in heaven.

This project of ecumenical dogmatics takes as its starting point the biblical history of promise and the principle of hope. Promise and hope point to a future beyond the present, expecting new things to happen. The focus is centered on the future of Jesus Christ as the Alpha and Omega, who was raised as the sovereign Lord of history to fulfill the promise of righteousness for all and as the gracious and wise judge of all the living and the dead. These few words and sentences formulate a preface for the following treatment of highly controversial issues in the history of Christian eschatology and today.

The parting words of Jesus to his disciples were: "Go therefore and make disciples of all nations, baptizing them in the name of the Father and of the Son and of the Holy Spirit, teaching them to observe all that I have commanded you; and lo, I am with you always, to the close of the age."[20] Here we have the word *all*, suggesting a universal perspective deeply grounded in the radical monotheism of biblical revelation. "Know therefore this day, and lay it to your heart, that the Lord is God in heaven and on the earth beneath; there is no other."[21] Isaiah declares that Israel's mission is to bring "justice to the nations"[22] and "light to the nations."[23] In addition Israel looked forward to the coming of a Messiah with power to redeem the world. In the New Testament the universal perspective trumps the narrow nationalistic ideology of the Zionists. Jesus said, "I tell you, many will come from east and west and sit at the table with Abraham, Isaac, and Jacob in the kingdom of heaven."[24] "Salvation is from the Jews,"[25] but the Apostle Paul's missionary journeys made it clear that salvation is for Gentiles as well, actually for all peoples, everywhere, until the end of time. One of the last things that Jesus told the disciples before his crucifixion was that "the gospel of the kingdom will be preached throughout the whole world, as a testimony to all nations; and then the end will come."[26] The mission of God is to save the whole of humanity, past, present, and future. The Savior has commissioned the church to carry out this mission, a particular means to accomplish a universal goal.

"God desires all people to be saved and to come to the knowledge of the truth."[27] The difficulty is that the means God has chosen (the church) to

20. Matthew 28:19–20.
21. Deuteronomy 4:39.
22. Isaiah 42:1.
23. Isaiah 42:6.
24. Matthew 8:11.
25. John 4:22b.
26. Matthew 24:14.
27. 1 Timothy 2:4.

reach the goal of salvation for all proves to be woefully inadequate. For one thing, what about all those who lived and died before the church came into existence? For another, what about the millions who have lived and died out of earshot of any oral proclamation of the gospel? The dogmatic tradition that promoted Augustine's view consigned the *mass damnata* to eternal punishment in hell. In the end God's intention to save everyone would be frustrated, allowing Satan's hell to receive the majority of God's creatures. A medieval church council stated Augustine's dark view without wincing: "The souls of those who depart this life in actual mortal sin, or in original sin alone go down straightaway to hell to be punished."[28] Some version of the Augustinian view has been taught by the majority of churches and theologians for centuries until a paradigm shift came to expression in the theologies of Karl Barth, Hans Urs von Balthasar, and Jürgen Moltmann, among others.

Their belief in universal salvation is not based on any kind of speculative metaphysics; rather, it is based on their interpretation of biblical texts. What texts? "God was in Christ, reconciling the world to himself."[29] Reconciliation in Christ is universal. Another text: ""We have an advocate with the Father, Jesus Christ the righteous, and he is the expiation for our sins, and not for ours only but also for the sins of the whole world."[30] The atoning work of Christ is universally efficacious. This passage contradicts the doctrine of limited atonement, the idea that Christ's atoning death benefits only the elect. Yet another text from a different angle: "Therefore God has highly exalted him and bestowed on him the name which is above every name, that at the name of Jesus every knee should bow, in heaven and on earth and under the earth, and every tongue confess that Jesus Christ is Lord, to the glory of God the Father."[31] "Every" means everybody living or dead, here or hereafter, on earth or in heaven.

Universalism has acquired an unsavory reputation as the teaching of heretics. The modern pluralistic theory of religions qualifies as a modern example of such heresy. In its view Christians may believe in Christ as their Savior, but other religions have their own savior figures. There are supposedly many

---

28. Quoted in MacDonald, ed., *"All Shall Be Well,"* 385.
29. 2 Corinthians 5:19a.
30. 1 John 2:1b–2.
31. Philippians 2:9–11.

13. ESCHATOLOGY: THE CHRISTIAN HOPE

roads that lead to God or whatever destiny each religion has to offer. Only the most narrow-minded bigotry of theological fundamentalism would supposedly still claim that Jesus Christ is God's way of salvation "once for all."[32] The neo-orthodox universalism of Barth, von Balthasar, and Moltmann, to the contrary, is based on a christocentric trinitarian monotheism of classical Christianity normed by the ancient creeds of the church. They do not claim church dogmatic status for their type of universalism. They concede that some biblical texts refer to hell, eternal damnation, and a final judgment that sorts out the sheep from the goats. Quoting biblical texts does not settle the issue, since there are texts that can be adduced in favor of eternal rejection as well as universal salvation. Arguments for one side or the other must necessarily remain tentative, since the subject in dispute is a matter of the eschatological future fully knowable only to God. Christians can know with certainty what they hope for and why. They can know what they pray for and why. Hope-filled prayer is not optimism or a pious wish for this or that. Christians do not hope and pray for their enemies to go to hell. Jesus said, "Love your enemies!"[33]

At best a case may be made for the possibility of universal salvation, an impossible possibility, not willing to sell short the power, wisdom, and love of God. The universalist hope is unquestionably a minority view in the history of Christianity, but that does not place it outside the pale of Christian orthodoxy. The fact that the majority of churches and theologians have taught the traditional doctrine of eternal damnation and hell does not close the matter for discussion. The majority is not always right. This possibility of universal salvation is advocated by Karl Barth, not often one accused of teaching heresy. "There is no good reason why we should forbid ourselves, or be forbidden, openness to the possibility that in the reality of God and man in Jesus Christ there is contained much more than we might expect and therefore the supremely unexpected withdrawal of that final threat, i.e., that in the truth of this reality there might be contained the super-abundant promise of the final deliverance of all people. To be more explicit, there is no good reason why we should not be open to this possibility . . . of an *apokatastasis* or universal reconciliation."[34]

---

32. Romans 6:10.
33. Matthew 5:44.
34. Barth, *Church Dogmatics*, IV/3, first half, 478.

Universalist hope is not a dogma of the church, nor are any of its alternatives. The rival eschatological doctrines of predestination (Reformed) or conditional election (Arminian) are both dualistic, envisioning a final victory for the devil and defeat of God's original plan. Eschatological theology remains controversial in church and theology. It is open to ongoing inquiry, never having been definitely treated in any dogmatic constitution of the church, ancient, medieval, or modern. Ordinary Christians, young and old, will continue to ask troublesome questions. Will God's mercy come to naught for the vast majority of the world's population who have never had a chance to hear the good news of the saving gospel of Jesus Christ? Will God's eternal love be nullified by his wrath or limited by human freedom? Is God bound by any external necessity that constrains his unconditional love? Will the justice of God trump his unconditional love in the end? Is there sufficient reason based on Scripture to negate what Barth writes:

> No aversion, rebellion or resistance on the part of non-Christians will be strong enough to resist the fulfillment of the promise of the Spirit which is pronounced over them too . . . to hinder the overthrow of their ignorance in the knowledge of Jesus Christ. . . . The stream is too strong and the dam too weak for us to be able reasonably to expect anything but the collapse of the dam and the onrush of the waters. In this sense Jesus Christ is the hope even of these non-Christians.[35]

Barth pins all his hope for the universal future of salvation on the death and resurrection of Christ. He does not believe that people are too good to be damned or that they may find an alternative way of salvation apart from Christ. The eternal destiny of all people is why Christ is necessary.

> There is not one for whose sin and death Christ did not die, whose sin and death he did not remove and obliterate on the cross. . . . There is not one who is not adequately and perfectly and finally justified in him. There is not one whose sin is not forgiven sin in him, whose death is not a death which had been put to death in him. . . . There is not one for whom he has not done everything in his death and received everything in his resurrection from the dead.[36]

---

35. Karl Barth, *Church Dogmatics*, IV/3, first half, 355–56.
36. Karl Barth, *Church Dogmatics*, IV/1, 638.

The Last Judgment

The Christian eschatological hope that in the end God will find a way to save all his creatures does not mitigate the severity of his judgment. Paul writes, "We must all appear before the judgment seat of Christ, so that each one may receive good or evil, according to what he has done in his body."[37] The Apostles' Creed confesses that Christ "will come to judge the living and the dead." His eschatological judgment is inescapable; no one will be exempt from his just verdict. This aspect of eschatology has been silenced in the pulpits of today, reminding one of the way H. Richard Niebuhr described the preaching of liberal Protestantism: "A God without wrath brought people without sin into a kingdom without judgment through the ministrations of a Christ without the cross."[38]

The last judgment is the time and occasion when God will expose all the evil, wickedness, and atrocities that have been committed in world history by individuals and nations. At the same time the final judgment may offer a post-mortem invitation to repentance, a necessary prerequisite to entering into the righteous kingdom of God. Everyone will be brought to realize that they are in the wrong, without excuse, and stand before the impartial judge. The author of Hebrews writes, "Before him no creature is hidden, but all are open and laid bare to the eyes of him with whom we have to do."[39] And in Romans Paul writes, "For it is written, 'As I live, says the Lord, every knee shall bow to me, and every tongue shall give praise to God.' So each of us shall give account of himself to God."[40] When? On the day of judgment! The idea of entering heaven without passing through the gate of judgment is an uninviting prospect. That would be like showing up on one's wedding day in dirty clothes, unbefitting the festive celebration. Judgment day is a time of reckoning with the truth about one's life in need of a savior and of recognizing the folly of saying "No" to God's final invitation of salvation.

Critics of universalism understandably ask, "So what then is the point of evangelism?" If everything is going to turn out all right, no matter what, why should the church bother to bear witness to the gospel of Jesus Christ

---

37. 2 Corinthians 5:10.
38. Niebuhr, *The Kingdom of God in America*, 193.
39. Hebrews 4:13.
40. Romans 14:11–12.

to those who don't give a hoot to hear it? What is the urgency? There is only one answer—because Jesus told his followers to do just that. How the many shall pass through the narrow gate is not something about which the Lord told his believers to worry. They have only to place their trust in God who will deal with the world according to his gracious word in Jesus Christ.

Questions for Discussion

1. Eschatology has to do with the end of the world, the last things. What is the reason Christian dogmatics deals with eschatology since no one has experienced or has any direct knowledge about future events that have not yet happened?
2. What does the Old Testament contribute to Christian thinking about eschatology?
3. Why is eschatological hope not utopian? What is the difference between hope for the coming of the kingdom of God and a longing for a utopian paradise on earth?
4. Modern theologians have produced different interpretations of eschatology that have to do with the various tenses of time. Identify three of them and describe how they are different and which is to be preferred from your perspective.
5. Christian theologians and traditions have different expectations about the final destiny of human beings—as different as hell and heaven and purgatory. Is there a sound biblical reason to think one way or another?
6. Universal hope for salvation has always been a thin stream in the Christian tradition, based on a few biblical passages. What is the reason for their hope?
7. The belief in the last judgment has been a part of Christian theology from the beginning. Such a belief seems to have waned in modern times, and is virtually absent in much of today's preaching. Do you think there are good reasons to retain this belief, and what is lost if it is abandoned?

Bibliography

Anderson, H. George, J. H. Stafford, and Joseph Burgess, eds. *The One Mediator, the Saints, and Mary*. Lutherans and Catholics in Dialogue VIII. Minneapolis: Augsburg, 1952.
"Apology of the Augsburg Confession." In *The Book of Concord*, translated and edited by Theodore G. Tappert, 232–33. Philadelphia: Fortress, 1959.
Aulén, Gustaf. *Christus Victor*. Translated by A. G. Herbert. New York: Macmillan, 1967.
Barth, Karl. *Church Dogmatics*. Vol. I/1. Translated by G. T. Thomson. New York: Scribner's Sons, 1936.
———. *Church Dogmatics*. Vol. IV/3, first half. Edited by Geoffrey W. Bromiley and Thomas F. Torrance. Edinburgh: T & T Clark, 1962.
———. *Epistle to the Romans*. Translated by Edwin C. Hoskyns. London: Oxford University Press, 1933.
Baur, Ferdinand Christian. *Die christliche Gnosis: Oder, Die christliche Religions-philosophie in ihrer geschichtlichen Entwicklung*. Tübingen, Germany: Osiander, 1835.
Benz, Ernst. "Ideas for a Theology of the History of Religions." In *The Theology of the Christian Mission*, edited by Gerald H. Anderson, 135–47. New York: McGraw Hill, 1961.
Bonhoeffer, Dietrich. *Letters and Papers from Prison*. Translated by Reginald H. Fuller. New York: Macmillan, 1953.
Braaten, Carl E. "Modern Interpretations of Nestorius." *Church History*, September 1963, 251–67.
Braaten, Carl E., and Roy A. Harrisville, eds. *Kerygma and History. A Symposium on the Theology of Rudolf Bultmann*. New York: Abingdon, 1962.
Braaten, Carl E., and Robert W. Jenson, eds. *Mary, Mother of God*. Grand Rapids: Eerdmans, 2004.
Braaten, Carl E., and Robert W. Jenson, eds. *Sin, Death, and the Devil*. Grand Rapids: Eerdmans, 2000.
Bultmann, Rudolf. *History and Eschatology*. Edinburgh: The University Press, 1957.
———. "The New Testament and Mythology." In *Kerygma and Myth*, edited by Hans-Werner Bartsch and translated by Reginald H. Fuller, 1–44. London: SPCK, 1954.
Catechism of the Catholic Church. New York: Doubleday, 1995.
Confessing the One Faith: An Ecumenical Explication of the Apostolic Faith as it is Confessed in the Nicene-Constantinopolitan Creed (381). Faith and Order Paper, No. 153. Geneva: WCC, 1991.
Cullmann, Oscar. *Christ and Time*. Translated by Floyd V. Filson. Philadelphia: Westminster, 1950.
Elert, Werner. *The Structure of Lutheranism*. Translated by Walter A. Hansen. St. Louis: Concordia, 1962.

BIBLIOGRAPHY

Forde, Gerhard O. *On Being a Theologian of the Cross: Reflections on Luther's Heidelberg Disputation*. Grand Rapids: Eerdmans, 1997.
"Formula of Concord, Solid Declaration, Article VII, The Person of Christ." In *The Book of Concord*, translated and edited by Theodore G. Tappert, 591–610. Philadelphia: Fortress, 1959.
Funk, Robert W. *Honest to Jesus*. New York: HarperCollins, 1996.
Griffin, David. *A Process Christology*. Philadelphia: Westminster, 1973.
Hick, John. *God Has Many Names*. Philadelphia: Westminster, 1980.
Hick, John, ed. *The Myth of God Incarnate*. Philadelphia: Westminster, 1977.
Hinlicky, Paul, and R. David Nelson. *Martyrdom and the Suffering of the Righteous*. New York: ALPB, 2015.
Hoeller, Stephen A. *Gnosticism: New Light on the Ancient Tradition of Inner Knowing*. Wheaton, IL: Theosophical Publishing House, 2002.
Holmes, Michael W., ed. "Letter to Diognetus." In *The Apostolic Fathers*, 2nd ed., translated by J. B. Lightfoot and J. R. Hammer, 296–306. Grand Rapids: Baker, 1989.
Jenson, Robert W. *Lutheran Slogans, Use and Abuse*. New York: ALPB, 2011.
John Paul II. *Ut Unum Sint: Encyclical Letter on Commitment to Ecumenism*. Vatican City: Liberia Editrice Vaticana, 1995.
Jonas, Hans. *The Gnostic Religion*. Boston: Beacon, 1958.
Kähler, Martin. *The So-Called Historical Jesus and the Historic Biblical Christ*. Translated by Carl E. Braaten. Philadelphia: Fortress, 1964.
Kasper, Walter. *The God of Jesus Christ*. Translated by Matthew J. O'Connell. New York: Crossroad, 1984.
Kaufman, Walter. "Existentialism and Death." In *The Meaning of Death*, edited by Herman Feifel, 39–63. New York: McGraw-Hill, 1959.
Knitter, Paul. *No Other Name?: A Critical Survey of Christian Attitudes Toward the World Religions*. Maryknoll, NY: Orbis, 1985.
Kraus, Hans Joachim. *Geschichte der historisch-kritischen Erforschung des Alten Testaments*. Neukirchen: Verlag der Buchhandlung des Erziehungsvereins, 1956.
Kuhn, Thomas. *The Structure of Scientific Revolutions*. Chicago: University of Chicago Press, 1970.
Küng, Hans. *Christianity and World Religions*. Translated by Peter Neinegg. Garden City, NY: Doubleday, 1986.
Lapide, Pinchas. *The Resurrection of Jesus: A Jewish Perspective*. Translated by Wilhelm Linss. Minneapolis: Augsburg Fortress, 1982.
Lee, Philip J. *Against the Protestant Gnostics*. New York: Oxford University Press, 1987.
Lessing, Gotthold Ephraim. *Nathan the Wise*. Translated by Günther Reinhardt. Brooklyn: Barrons Educational Series, 1950.
"Letter to Diognetus." In *The Apostolic Fathers*, 2d ed., translated by J. B. Lightfoot and J. R. Hammer, edited and revised by Michael W. Holmes, 291–306. Grand Rapids: Baker, 1989.
Loisy, Alfred. *The Gospel and the Church*. Translated by Bernhard B. Scott. Philadelphia: Fortress, 1976.
Lüdemann, Gerd. *The Resurrection of Jesus: History, Experience, Theology*. Philadelphia: Fortress, 1994.
Luther, Martin. "Against the Antinomians." *Luther's Works*, vol. 47, 99–118. Philadelphia: Fortress, 1971.

———. *Lectures on Galatians 1–4. Luther's Works: American Edition* vol. 26. St. Louis: Concordia, 1963.
———. "The Magnificat." *Luther's Works*, vol. 21, 295–358. St. Louis: Concordia, 1956.
———. *Martin Luthers Werke, Kritische Gesamtausgabe, XXVII*. Weimar, 1883.
———. "On the Councils and the Church." *Luther's Works*, vol. 41, 3–178. Philadelphia: Fortress, 1971.
———. "The Large Catechism." In *The Book of Concord*, translated and edited by Theodore Tappert, 357–461. Philadelphia: Fortress, 1959.
———. "The Smalcald Articles." In *The Book of Concord*, translated and edited by Theodore Tappert, 287–318. Philadelphia: Fortress, 1959.
———. "The Small Catechism." In *The Book of Concord*, translated and edited by Theodore Tappert, 337–356. Philadelphia: Fortress, 1959.
———. "Solid Declaration," Article VII, The Person of Christ. In *The Book of Concord*, translated and edited by Theodore Tappert, 591–610. Philadelphia: Fortress, 1959.
MacDonald, Gregory, ed. *"All Shall Be Well": Explorations in Universal Salvation and Christian Theology from Origen to Moltmann*. Eugene, OR: Cascade, 2011.
Melanchthon, Philip. "Apology of the Augsburg Confession." In *The Book of Concord*, translated and edited by Theodore Tappert, 97–285. Philadelphia: Fortress, 1959.
———. *Loci Communes*. Translated by J. A. O. Preus. St. Louis: Concordia, 1992.
Moltmann, Jürgen. *The Crucified God*. Translated by R. A. Wilson and John Bowden. Minneapolis: Fortress, 1993.
———. *The Trinity and the Kingdom*. Translated by Margaret Kohl. Minneapolis: Fortress, 1993.
Niebuhr, H. Richard. "The Doctrine of the Trinity and the Unity of the Church." *Theology Today* 3 (1946) 371–84.
———. *The Kingdom of God in America*. New York: Harper, 1959.
Newbigin, Lesslie. "The Enduring Validity of Cross-Cultural Mission." *International Bulletin of Missionary Research* 12.2 (October–December 1988) 50–53.
———. *Trinitarian Faith and Today's Mission*. Richmond, VA: Knox, 1963.
Ogden, Schubert. *Christ Without Myth*. New York: Harper, 1961.
O'Regan, Cyril. *Gnostic Return in Modernity*. Albany, NY: State University New York Press, 2001.
Origins. CNS Documentary Service, Vol. 23, No. 29. January 6, 1994.
Owen, D. R. G. *Body and Soul*. Philadelphia: Westminster, 1956.
Polak, F. L. *The Image of the Future*. Translated by Elise Boulding. Leyden, the Netherlands: A. W. Sijthoff, 1961.
Prenter, Regin. *Spiritus Creator*. Translated by J. Jenson. Philadelphia: Fortress, 1953.
Rahner, Karl. *The Trinity*. Translated by Joseph Donceel. New York: Herder & Herder, 1970.
Robinson, John A. T. *The Body: A Study in Pauline Theology*. London: SCM, 1952.
Russell, Jeffrey Burton. *Mephistopheles: The Devil in the Modern World*. Ithaca, NY: Cornell University Press, 1986.
Sartre, Jean-Paul. "The Body." In *The Philosophy of the Body: Rejections of Cartesian Dualism*, edited by S. F. Spicker, 218–40. Chicago: Quadrangle, 1970.
Schleiermacher, Friedrich. *The Christian Faith*. Edited by H. R. Mackintosh and J. S. Stewart. Edinburgh: T & T Clark, 1928.
Schweitzer, Albert. *The Quest of the Historical Jesus*. Translated by N. Montgomery. London: Black, 1910.

BIBLIOGRAPHY

Schlink, Edmund. "After the Council." In *Ecumenical and Confessional Writings*, vol. 1, translated and edited by Matthew L. Becker, 239–536. Göttingen, Germany: Vandenhoek & Ruprecht, 2017.

Schmid, Heinrich. *Doctrinal Theology of the Evangelical Lutheran Church*. Translated by Charles A. Hay and Henry E. Jacobs. Minneapolis: Augsburg, 1961.

Sellers, R. V. *The Council of Chalcedon*. London: SPCK, 1953.

Skillrud, Harold C., J. Francis Stafford, and Daniel Martensen, eds. *Lutherans and Catholics in Dialogue 9*. Minneapolis: Augsburg Fortress, 1995.

Smoley, Richard. *Forbidden Faith: The Secret History of Gnosticism*. San Francisco: HarperCollins, 2006.

Strauss, David Friedrich. *The Life of Jesus Critically Examined*. Edited by Peter Hodgson. Philadelphia: Westminster, 1972.

Tillich, Paul. "Der Begriff des Dämonischen und sein Bedeutung für systematische Theologie." *Theologische Blätter* 5 (February 1926) 32–35.

Tournier, Paul. "Preface." In *The Meaning of the Body*, edited by J. Sarano, 16. Translated by J. H. Farley. Philadelphia: Westminster, 1966.

Voegelin, Eric. *Science, Politics, and Gnosticism*. Wilmington, DE: ISI, 2004.

Wedderburn, A. J. M. *Beyond Resurrection*. Peabody, MA: Hendrickson, 1999.

Wittgenstein, Ludwig. *Philosophical Investigations*, part IV. New York: Macmillan, 1953.

Index

Abelard, 73
absolution, 105-5
adiaphora, 110
Adoptionism, 57, 60, 63
Adventists, 113
Alexandrian Theology, 58-60, 69
Altizer, Thomas J. J., 24
Anglican Church, ix, 97, 133
Anonymous Christ, 19
Anselm, 23, 72-73
Antichrist, 48
antinomianism, 29, 41
Antiochian Theology, 58-60, 69
Apollinaris, 59
Apostles' Creed, ix-x, xvi, 65, 74, 86, 88, 155
Apostolic church/faith, xviii, 106
Aquinas, xv, 18, 23, 93, 121, 123
Aristotle, xv, 23, 44, 126
Arius/Arianism 10, 59
Arminius/Arminianism 6, 40
Areopagus, 22,136
atonement, xvii, 40, 72-74
Athanasius, x, 10, 13, 59
Athanasian Creed, ix-x, xvi
Augsburg Confession, xviii, 99
Augustine, xv, 10, 13, 18, 37-39, 41-42, 72, 93, 102, 104, 116-17, 121, 136, 152
Aulén, Gustaf, 74

Baptism, xvii-xviii, xix, 95, 104-9
Barth, Karl, xviii, 4, 6, 12, 16, 20, 38, 80,146-47, 149, 152-54
Baur, Ferdinand C., 41-42
Baptism, Eucharist and Ministry (Lima Text), 99, 105-6, 110

Becker, Ernst, 43
Bergson, Henri, 28
Borg, Marcus, 5
Bernanos, Georges, 46-47
Biel, Gabriel, 40
body, 30-31, 78-79
Bonaventure, 18, 121
Bonhoeffer, Dietrich, 24, 71
Brunner, Emil, 38
Bultmann, Rudolf, 6, 30, 66, 78, 148-49
Buddha/Buddhism, xiii, 134, 137, 140

Calvin, John, xviii, 9, 13, 18, 38, 68, 95, 121
Canon, biblical, xvi, 97
Carpocrates, 29
Charismatic churches/movement, 85, 9
Chemnitz, Martin, 3
Christian unity, x, 15
Christology, xvii, 50-52, 57-63, 66, 83, 134
church, xvii, 9, 15, 90-99, 118, 120, 126, 134
Clement of Alexandria, xv
Clement of Rome, 56
conscience, 21, 117, 121
Copernican Revolution, 12, 93
Council of Trent, 3, 104
Councils of the Church, xvi, 58
creation out of nothing, 26-27
Creator/creation, xvi, 10, 28-30, 41, 56, 120-23, 136
Creed of Chalcedon, 51, 55, 60-61
Crossan, John D., 5, 77
cross and resurrection, 19, 76
Cross of Christ, 53, 56, 70-75, 136, 140
Cullmann, Oscar, 6, 30, 148-49

161

INDEX

Cyprian, 15
Cyrus, 117

Dalai Lama, 140
Darwin, Charles, 28, 30
Day, Dorothy, 121
Dead Sea Scrolls, 36
death, 42–45, 55, 143–47, 150
death and resurrection, 28, 45, 48, 53–56, 69, 79, 132
de Beauvoir, Simone, 42
Decalogue, 125
de Chardin, Teilhard, 28
Deism, 14
Derrida, Jacques, xv
Descartes, René, xv, 23
demythologize, 66, 78
Descent into hell, 65, 75
Devil, 42, 45–48, 66, 72
Diocletian, xv
Docetism, 30, 57, 63
dogma/dogmatics, xii-xvii, 4, 37, 47, 66, 112, 150
Dodd, C. H., 148–49

Easter, 56, 74, 77
Ebionitism, 57, 63
ecology, 32, 119
economy, 120–24
ecumenical dogmatics, xiii, 60, 150
ecumenical movement, xii, xix, 2, 91, 109, 132
Eddy, Mary Baker, x, xiii, 41
Elert, Werner, 28
Enlightenment, 11, 23, 62, 134
Eros, 126
eschatology, xvii, 114, 141, 143–56
eternal life, 104, 108
ethics, 124–1255
eutyches/Eutycheanism, 60
Evangelical Catholics, xi, xvii-xviii, 7
Evangelization, 131–33, 139
evil, 27, 31, 38, 46–47
evolution, 28, 38
experience, xii, 37
external Word, 101–2

faith, xiii, 6, 30, 40, 88, 112, 115, 143
Feuerbach, Ludwig, 24, 30
Fichte, Johann G., xv
filioque, 9, 83, 86
Fiorenza, Elizabeth S., 91
First Vatican Council, 98
Florovsky, Georges, 91
forgiveness of sins, 68, 87, 104, 110–11, 116–17, 148
Fortes, Bruno, 91
Francis, Saint, 93, 102, 119, 124
Francke, Auguste H., 40
freedom, xvii, 34, 131
free will, 26, 40
Freud, Sigmund, 30, 44, 125
Fundamentalism, 5, 66
Funk, Robert, 77

German idealism, 42
gospel, x, xiii, xvii-xviii, 13, 16, 18, 41, 66, 84–85, 88, 90, 96, 98–99, 106, 117–18, 120, 128, 130, 132, 135–36, 147
Gnosticism, xv, 31, 41, 60, 95
grace, 34, 40, 128
Gregory of Nyssa, 72
Griffin, David, 78
Grünewald, Mathias, 70
Gunton, Colin, 12

Hamilton, William, 24
Hartshorne, Charles, xv
heaven, 45, 65–66, 79, 150
Heidegger, Martin, xv
hell, 45, 65–66
Hellenization of the gospel, 136–37
heresy, xvi, 27, 29, 95, 132
hermeneutics, x, 6
Herrmann, Wilhelm, 11
Hinduism, 134, 137, 139
Hippolytus, 29, 95
historical criticism, xv, 6
historical Jesus, 5, 51, 78
Hitler, Adolf, 46, 81
hope, 143–45, 154–55
Hume, David, xv

INDEX

Immaculate Conception of Mary, 69–70
immortality of the soul, 30
incarnate Word, xi, 101
incarnation, 60–61, 117
Irenaeus, 13, 29, 95
Israel, xii

James, Letter of, xvi
Jenson, Robert W., 12
Jesus Seminar, 5, 77
Joachim, Abbot of Fiore, 84
John, Gospel of, xvi
judgment, 141, 147, 149, 155–56
justice, 118, 120, 131
justification by faith, xiii, xix, 104, 114–16, 149
Justin, Martyr, 22

Kähler, Martin, 5
Kant, Immanuel, xv, 11, 23
Kaufman, Walter, 43
kerygma, 14, 52, 94, 149
King, Martin Luther, 118, 121
kingdom of God, 52–56, 76, 87–88, 90, 114, 119, 128, 148–49
knowledge of God, xvii, 18
Knitter, Paul, 15
Küng, Hans, 76
Kuhn, Thomas, 11

LaCugna, Catherine, 12
Lapide, Pinchas, 76
last judgment, 141, 147, 149
law, 36, 114–18
law and gospel, 20–21, 102–4, 136
Leibniz, Gottfried, xv, 23, 27
Lessing, Gotthold E., 134
Letter to Diognetus, 116
Lewis, C. S., 45–46, 54
Liberal Protestantism, 11, 41, 73, 155
libido, 126
liturgical movement, 109
Logos, 11, 22–23, 59, 63, 67, 136
Loisy, Alfred, 90
Lord's Supper, xvii, 44, 53, 104–112
love, 115, 119, 125–27, 140
Lüdemann, Gerd, 78

Luther, Martin, xiv-xviii, 13, 6, 9, 13, 20–21, 24, 28, 39–41, 45, 45, 47, 62, 68–72, 80, 84–85. 87–88, 91, 93, 95, 98, 101–2, 104, 108–9, 112, 115, 121–23, 127
Lutherans, Lutheranism, ix, xviii, 40, 70, 94, 99, 133

Marcion, 29
Manichaeanism, 41
marriage, 124–28
Mary/Mariology/Mariolatry, 67–7
Mauriac, François, 46
McLuhan, Marshall, 66
means of grace, vii, 102, 105
Melanchthon, Philip, 3, 68, 99, 104–5
Menninger, Karl, 34
Merton, Thomas, 140
ministry, offices of, xviii, 96, 98, 100
mission of the church, missionary movement, missionaries, 15–16, 77, 96, 98, 130–39
Möhler, Adam, 91
Mohammed/Muslims, xiii, 137–39
Moltmann, Jurgen, 12, 76, 91, 146, 152–53
Monarchianism, 10, 39, 58
Montanus, Montanism, 83
Müntzer, Thomas, 101
mythology, xv, 65–66

Neubigin, Lesslie, 15
Nestorius/Nestorianism, 59, 63, 140
Nicene Creed, ix, xiv, 9,11,16, 56, 83, 86, 94–95
Niebuhr, H. Richard, 14, 155
Niebuhr, Reinhold, 38
Niemöller, Martin, 81
Nietzsche, Friedrich, 24, 30

Ockham, William, xv
Ogden, Schubert, 77
ordination, 98–99
Origen, xv, 18, 53, 72, 121
original sin, 37–39
Orthodoxy, Eastern, 9, 47, 83–84, 91–92, 97, 104–5, 132–33

INDEX

Osiander, Andreas, 4

Pannenberg, Wolfhart, 12, 30, 38, 76, 91, 146
pantheism, 26
Papal infallibility, Papal office, xix, 97–98
Pascal, Blaise, 24
Patripassionsim, 10, 57–58, 60
Paul of Samosata, 57
peace, xvii, 118, 120, 131, 134–35
Péguy, Antoine, 46
Pelagius, Pelagianism, 39–40, 58
Pentecost, 90, 135, 149
Pentecostals, Pentecostalism, 85, 105, 133
Pharisees, 37, 75
philia, 126
philosophy, xv, 21
Plato/Platonism, 23, 30, 44, 126
Plotinus, 31, 145
pluralistic theology of religions, 15–16, 22, 133
Pontifical Biblical Commission, 6
Pope Pius XII, 28
Pope John XXIII, ix
Pope John Paul II, 92, 132
powers and principalities, xii, 48
preachers/preaching, 52, 102–3
Protestant Churches/Protestantism ix–x, 3, 47, 105, 132
purgatory, 45

Quenstedt, Johann, 4
Qu'ran, 138

Rahner, Karl, 11, 91, 146
reason, 6, 50. 117, 120
Reformation, 1, 3–4, 95, 98, 102, 104, 109
Reformed Church/ Reformed Confession, ix, 9
religions, 71, 77, 86, 134, 137–41
Renan, Ernst, 5
resurrection, 42, 47, 50, 55, 65, 65, 75–79, 101, 104, 108, 11b, 132, 143
revelation, xii, xiv, xvii, 6, 18–19, 66, 117, 120, 137, 14
Ritschl, Albrecht, 11
Robinson, John A.T., 24, 30

Roman Catholic Church/Roman Catholics ix, xi, xviii-xix, 2, 6, 47, 65, 69–70, 73, 91–92, 97, 104–5, 127, 132
Russell, Charles, xi

Sabellius/Sabellianism, 57–58, 60
sacraments, xvii, 7, 79, 85, 98–99, 101, 104–112, 127
salvation, 19, 21, 40–41, 55, 58–59, 66, 69, 103, 107, 120, 132, 137–40, 148–54
sanctification, 21, 108
Sartre, Jean-Paul, 31, 42
Sayers, Dorothy, xii
Schaff, Philip, 40
Schleiermacher, Friedrich, xi, 11, 46, 58
Schelling, Friedrich, xv
Schlink, Edmund, xiii, 38, 92
Schweitzer, Albert, 5, 147–49
Scotus, Duns, 23, 40
Scriptures,Holy, x, xvi, 1, 5, 9, 18, 87–88, 101, 125, 138, 143
Session at the Right Hand of God, 79–81
sex, 124–28
sin/sinners, 21, 33–40, 128
sin, death, and the devil, 19, 28, 33, 48, 67, 73–75
Smith, Joseph, xi, xiii
Socrates, 44
soul, 29–31
Spinoza, Benedictus de, xv
Spirit, Holy, ix, xvi, xix, 1–2, 4, 6, 10, 12, 14, 16, 40–41, 53, 83–88, 130, 133, 149
Strauss, David F., 5, 78
Stühlmacher, Peter, 76

Temple, William, 31
Ten Commandments, 104
Tertullian, xv, 29, 83, 95
theodicy, xvii, 27–28
theology of the cross, 70–72, 133
theology of glory, 70–72
theotokos, 68
Thomasius, Gottfried, 62–63
Tillich, Paul, 30, 46, 146

tongues, 85, 96
Torah, 76
Tournier, Paul, 31
tradition, xiii, xviii, 2–3, 33, 62
Trinity/trinitarian, ix, xiv, xvi, 9–17, 26, 51, 54, 57, 83, 87, 107, 130, 138

Unitarianism, 14, 58–59
universal salvation, 150–55
Ut Unum Sint, 92, 132

Valla, Lorenzo, x
Vatican Council II, ix, xix, 91, 97, 106
Vincent of Lérins/VincentianCanon, xviiii, 94
Virgin Birth, 67–69
Virgin Mary, 10, 58, 68, 86, 127
Voegelin, Eric, 42

von Balthasar, Hans Urs, 152–53
Von Harnack, Adolf, 11, 29

Ware, Kallistos, 12
Wedderburn, A. J. M. 77
Westminster Confession, 93
Whitehead, Alfred North, xv
Wittgenstein, Ludwig, xv
Word and Sacraments, 21, 98–99, 101–112
Word of God, xi, xiv, 1–4, 6, 23, 51, 87, 149
World Council of Churches, xviii, 85, 105
worship, 51, 118

Zizioulas, John, 12, 91
Zwingli, Huldreich, 62, 80, 109, 111, 127